Enhancing the Wellbeing and Wisdom of Older Learners

GW00546531

Enhancing the Wellbeing and Wisdom of Older Learners: A co-research paradigm examines how lifelong learning, becoming wise and sharing wisdom are integrally linked to older people's wellbeing. The book highlights appropriate learning styles and pedagogies for older people, including research models emphasising participation, and offers recommendations for research in lifelong learning with the potential to effect change.

Focusing upon a collaborative action research project, 'Sagaciation', chapters explore the involvement of older learners in the design and delivery of the scheme, which enabled them to expand their knowledge and skills and to fully engage as critical and creative voices in a supportive and welcoming environment. The book offers an account of the process of the action research, as well as its findings. The project is set into the context of leading academic thinking on fields such as the growth of an ageing population, the rise of literature on ageing, negative and positive constructions of ageing, social gerontology, the wellbeing and health of older people and educational gerontology.

This book challenges negative representations of older people as a burden by offering a paradigm of hope, resilience and sagacity within education and beyond. It will appeal to researchers, academics and postgraduate students in the fields of adult education, lifelong learning, gerontology, mental health and wellbeing and the sociology of education, as well as to policymakers and those working with older people.

Tess Maginess is Senior Lecturer in Education in the School of Education, Queen's University Belfast, Ireland, where much of her work is with older learners. Tess has been awarded a National Teaching Fellowship, has been shortlisted for the Aonatas 'STAR' awards for her research project 'Sagaciation' and previously won the BERA-SAGE Research Practitioner of the Year for Adult Education. She has published on literature, education and mental health.

Routledge Research in Lifelong Learning and Adult Education Series

Books in this series:

Enhancing the Wellbeing and Wisdom of Older Learners

A co-research paradigm

Tess Maginess

Routledge
Taylor & Francis Group

LONDON AND NEW YORK

First published 2017 by Routledge

2 Park Square, Milton Park, Abingdon, Oxfordshire OX14 4RN
711 Third Avenue, New York, NY 10017

Routledge is an imprint of the Taylor & Francis Group, an informa business

First issued in paperback 2017

British Library Cataloguing in Publication Data
A catalogue record for this book is available from the British Library

Library of Congress Cataloging-in-Publication Data
Names: Maginess, Tess, author.
Title: Enhancing the wellbeing and wisdom of older learners :
    a co-research paradigm / Tess Maginess.
Description: New York, NY : Routledge, 2016. | Series: Routledge
    research in lifelong learning and adult education series ; 4 |
    Includes bibliographical references and index.
Identifiers: LCCN 2016003132 | ISBN 9781138936775 (hardcover) |
    ISBN 9781315676623 (electronic)
Subjects: LCSH: Older people—Education—Psychological aspects. |
    Older people—Mental health. | Learning, Psychology of, in old
    age. | Educational psychology.
Classification: LCC LC5457 .M34 2016 | DDC 374—dc23
LC record available at https://lccn.loc.gov/2016003132

ISBN: 978-1-138-93677-5 (hbk)
ISBN: 978-0-8153-5721-6 (pbk)

Typeset in Sabon
by Apex CoVantage, LLC

This book is dedicated to the memory of June Smart and June McIlroy, whose lively and wise spirits have guided us.

Contents

Preface

This piece of research began when my estimable colleague, Wendy Hunter, administrator of the Open Learning Programme at Queen's University, Belfast, suggested that we should find out a bit more about what our learners thought about the programme. And, as I had carried out a number of projects with learners where they occupied a central role as co-participants in the research, I thought this would be the most organic way to conduct the research and to empower learners.

The aim of the study was to find out whether participation in the Open Learning Programme enhanced the wellbeing and wisdom of older learners. That might seem a simple enough question, which might yield a simple 'yes' by way of an answer. But, as you will see, the data reveals a much more complex response, for it is not just the 'why' of learning but the 'how' that makes the difference to students.

The broader aim of the study was to challenge negative stereotyping of older people as decrepit or a burden, and, as you will see, the work of the learners as co-researchers certainly challenges so unimaginative a mythology, for these older learners brought to the project their altruism, their enthusiasm, their skills, their experience, their openness and, again and again, their wisdom. And it seems many developed new skills, new perspectives and challenged some internal myths about ageing.

As we will see, older learners engaged in the project in a variety of ways from the outset. Some attended a special series of courses on ageing and gave us their feedback, others kindly agreed to sit on the steering group, others helped with the organisation and logistics, others participated as interviewers and interviewees and two students, Jane McComb and Charles Brannigan, acted as creative documenters. Two master's students from the School of Sociology, Social Policy and Social Work gave valuable assistance as interviewers and as data analysts. A little later, another master's student from the School of Education, Asma Niazi, joined the team, providing valuable assistance with the literature review, and in the final stages of preparing the research for publication, Dr Pauline Prior, an Open Learning Programme student and a former senior lecturer in the School of Sociology, Social Policy and Social Work, offered tremendous expertise in editing. Throughout the whole project, Allen Young, another Open Learning Programme student, worked with me unstintingly, participating in the interview process, working on the data analysis, contributing much to the literature review and, with Pauline and Asma, providing an eagle-eyed critique over several drafts of this book.

Colleagues from the School of Education, Aideen Gildea and Dr Laura Dunne, gave their valuable time and expertise in the early shaping of the project.

During the course of the research, we read a great deal of literature about older people and older people's learning, and I am truly indebted to the many wonderful experts for the learned framework they offer across a wide range of fields, from educational gerontology to cultural studies to economics to anthropology, social sciences and the arts. I wish also to express my thanks to Queen's University librarian Norma Menabney, who offered training to Allen Young and myself and who generously assisted with sourcing even the most obscure references.

Other colleagues in the university were also most helpful, especially Stephen Mullan from the audio-visual unit, who filmed the special courses. I also wish to pay tribute to the tutors who facilitated the special courses, Dr Cathal McManus and Aideen Gildea, and peer tutors Dr Michael Scott and Dr Cecilia Ward.

Very sadly, during the course of this project, two most valued participants, June Smart and June McIlroy, passed from this life. And we all agreed that the book should be dedicated to them. Their spouses, Ronnie Smart and Duncan McIlroy, very kindly consented to this.

In conclusion, I wish to express my heartfelt thanks to all those who made this project such a joy to work on. The many faults of the book must be laid entirely at my own door. I can only hope, however, that readers will share the pleasure of these older learners and learn, as I did, from their wisdom.

Acknowledgements

Many, many people have made this book possible. I wish to thank especially Allen Young, Pauline Prior and Asma Naizi, whose contribution to the literature review and editing of this book was as skilled as it was generous in spirit. I am deeply indebted also to all the students who gave so generously of their time in such a variety of ways. Thanks are due to university colleagues Aideen Gildea and Laura Dunne for their work on the early stages of the research, fellow tutors Cathal McManus, Carlo Gebler and Aideen Gildea, peer tutors Dr Michael Scott and Dr Cecilia Ward, librarian Norma Menabney and the staff of the audio-visual unit. I also wish to thank Professor John Gardner, University of Stirling, for his unfailing support over many years and specifically for his judicious comments on the book proposal. Thanks also to Dr Briege Casey, Dublin City University, and Professor Brian Findsen, University of Waikato, New Zealand, for their most helpful critiques. And my thanks are also due to the Open Learning team for all their support.

Finally, I would like to thank my patient and noble husband, Ian Maginness, who has held my hand in the worst of times and in the best of times.

List of participants

Steering group

Ms Adrianne Brown, Open Learning Programme student and secretary to Bangor U3A

Professor Sir George Bain, Open Learning Programme student and former vice-chancellor of Queen's University, Belfast

Ms Deborah Coleman, School of Nursing and Midwifery, Queen's University, Belfast

Dr Laura Dunne, Researcher, School of Education, Queen's University, Belfast

Professor John Gardner, Deputy Principal, University of Stirling

Ms Aideen Gildea, Researcher, School of Education, Queen's University, Belfast

Dr Eamonn Hughes, School of English, Queen's University, Belfast

Dr Maeve Rea, School of Medicine (Gerontology), Queen's University, Belfast

Dr Ian Rushton, School of Education and Professional Development, University of Huddersfield

Dr Michael Scott, Open Learning Programme student

Dr Joan Rahilly, School of English, Queen's University, Belfast

Ms Deborah Coleman, School of Nursing, Queen's University, Belfast

Interviewers and interviewees

George Bain	Dilys Harkins
Charles Brannigan	Irene Harper
Maureen Brown	Jay Holmes
Mae Burke	June Jordan

Deirdre Kennedy	Liam Parker
John Knox	Ruth Rankin
Marilyn Humphrey	Joan Semple
Bill Love	June Smart (RIP)
Pat Love	Trevor Walker
Denise Lynch	Cecilia Ward
Duncan McIlroy	Isabelle Weir
June McIlroy (RIP)	Allen Young

Creative documenters

Charles Brannigan (illustrations)

Ian Maginess (photograph)

Jane McComb (photographs)

Peer tutors

Dr Michael Scott

Dr Cecilia Ward

Data analysts and editors

Asma Naizi

Dr Pauline Prior

Allen Young

Chapter 1

Introduction

What this book is about

This book is not about how to grow old gracefully, invisibly or scandalously. It is about what some older learners think being involved in an adult education programme means for them and what it might mean for other older people. Their views, their voices, were articulated through a research project conducted among older learners involved in Queen's University's adult education Open Learning Programme. The programme had its foundations in the 1850s, attracts some 6,000 enrolments each year and offers a wide variety of courses.

The central question of the research project conducted with older learners was, 'does participation in education enhance your wellbeing?' The book is based on research conducted with rather than to or at older learners. It is a co-research project. Their voices cause and shape this book. As we will see in a later chapter, co-research conducted by students is still rare enough and research conducted by older students is even rarer.

Older learners were involved at every stage and in all manners. From participation in the research project steering group to becoming planners, logicians, interviewees, interviewers, data analysts, creative documenters, researchers, editors and writers, older learners have enacted a model of co-research through which they have – sometimes quietly and firmly, sometimes with brio, sometimes with wry humour – challenged negative stereotyping and demonstrated, on their own terms, how participation in learning can enhance wellbeing. It is to be hoped that this book will contribute to that research and that readers will be able to draw from it practical lessons on not only how to improve programmes but also how to engage older learners as co-researchers. And it is to be hoped, above all, that this book will be for policymakers a very positive demonstration of the benefits of older people learning and how, as a result, greater focus and greater funding can be trained on how to improve access and participation for older people. While the subject is older people's learning and research, the broader concept is about empowering older people to contribute, capably, wisely and far more fully to society through a whole range of domains: business, the arts, health, housing, the environment and politics. We hope that the book may provide some practical modelling as well as a theoretical context for the generation of dynamic and innovative thinking about older people, locally, regionally, nationally and internationally.

Definitions: wellbeing, wisdom, sagacity, sagaciation

But what do we mean by terms like wellbeing, wisdom and 'sagacity'? And can the acquisition of wisdom be viewed as a process – that we might term 'sagaciation'? Let's start with 'wellbeing'.

Wellbeing

Perhaps the simplest meaning of that word is what used to be called 'content-ment'. As Roberts (2012, p. 13) acknowledges, this is a term that has a very wide range of meanings and uses, but she helpfully informs us that 'in the growing body of international research', wellbeing has to do with how an older person can develop resilience, 'handle adversity and build a promising life'. As we will see, wellbeing has to do not only with an individual's attitude but also with how societies frame their attitude to older people and, consequently, how they make it more or less difficult for older people to attain wellbeing.

Wisdom

Again, this is a word which people understand in all sorts of different ways, but interestingly, it is not a word that is used so very much in current parlance. It would take another book entirely to explain why this is, but perhaps the word 'wisdom' *carries with it connotations of authority and paternalism or even maternalism, which are deeply inimical in the contemporary world. Conventional, historical representations of older people as, by virtue of their age, wise are countered by as many representations portraying older people as fond, foolish, outrageous or irrelevant. Age does not necessarily confer wisdom, as Sternberg (2005, p. 6) confirms, but it can.* In another contribution to the topic, Sternberg and Grigorenko (2005, p. 214) also stress the value of wisdom – more wise ideas should survive over time in a culture than unwise ideas. And, for these authors, wisdom includes virtue – the desire for a good state or condition – for the common good, an imperative we will return to shortly.

Sagacity, sagaciation

The association between wisdom, or sagacity and older people has been questioned over cultures and history, in terms of not only whether older age automatically confers sagacity but also whether such a quality, such an attribute, is important to society. So, perhaps the question is not about some recognisable, immemorial tussle between the relative clichéd merits and deficiencies of youth and age but rather how people of every age have the capacity to teach and learn. What comes across very strongly in the research conducted with and by older learners is that the acquisition of knowledge and wisdom is, above all, a process and a process that exposes them, sometimes in quite a sheer fashion, to what they do not know and want to or need to learn. In other words, learning, just as with young people, is a process, a journey, a voyage.

For older people this process is about combining what they know with what they do not know. Older people who engage with learning, with education, are not only capable of learning but also keen to learn. And, as the findings of this research project reveal, older learners are engaged in a very definite process of becoming wise through, crucially, their own openness to learning. And that process is not simply about their own journey, their own self-actualisation, but also about how other older people could be enabled to have a bit of fun, defy a cliché or two, and quietly learn some skill or knowledge they always had a yen for or have just discovered as something worth bothering about.

I call this process 'sagaciation' – making wise. And it would seem that in the making of wisdom, humour might just occur. I did not invent this term – my ancestors did, through a rhyme they made when they met among the hills and forests and loughs in a remote and lively part of Ulster:

> How do you sagaciate?
> Quite rumbumptious, up to date.

They made up the word, irreverently, arising from a basic education away back in the early 1900s, where Latin inflected English in a way that it does not now. But their question has a certain potency for our topic and for our time; to 'sagaciate' meant to be up to date, somehow, with the wider world, and also, to be a little bit irreverent too; there is an energetic and comic defiance of accepted norms, of received wisdom and, perhaps, we may add, of received wisdom about how wisdom actually operates among older people, how they sagaciate. And it seems to me that the results of the research we conducted with older learners are also 'quite rumbumptious and up to date' in challenging, for our time, some received ideas about older people and how they actually think and feel. Much terrific research has been done in new fields, like educational gerontology, but not so much of it has been based upon directly involving older people themselves as active participants, as co-researchers. This book presents their unvarnished views about their experience not only as learners but also as active researchers, and in that very process, as people involved in a process of sagaciation, of making wise, but ultimately as sagaciators, people who teach us how to learn.

Is sagaciation integral to wellbeing among older people – and to us all?

I believe that it is. Being involved in a process of sagaciation involves an openness to learn and to reflect on how and why we learn. Again and again, the research conducted by older learners emphasises their enthusiasm, their delight in learning. As a consequence, their image of themselves is positive and optimistic and hence their sense of wellbeing is enhanced.

Engaging in a continual, lifelong process of becoming wise empowers older people to feel more in control of their lives, to be active rather than passive and to build the resilience to deal with the difficult and challenging life situations they are destined to face. Our research demonstrates that they are keen to get this message out, to encourage older people not currently engaged in learning to get involved. And beyond that, the research reveals how much older people want to feel valued, want to be an asset to society. This book affords a glimpse into the great potential of older people to offer us all a model of wisdom and wellbeing. There is much that we can all learn.

The importance of considering the potential of older people: the 'agequake'

But why focus on older people in the first place? Why is a book like this needed or relevant? Ageing and older people are becoming huge global topics for our time. And this is primarily because of changing demography. Let us then have a look at the statistics before going on to consider how society views or 'constructs' older people.

An expanding older population: the statistics

It is now a truth universally acknowledged that we have an expanding older population, globally. Experts in the emerging field of educational gerontology drew attention to the changing UK demography over 20 years ago (Withnal and Percy, 1994; Beatty and Wolf, 1996). Beatty and Wolf (1996, p. 5) argued that '60% of the projected increase in numbers of households between 2008 and 2033 will be headed by someone aged 65 or over'. More recently, Roberts has reported on what has been termed the 'agequake'. According to the figures she cites, by 2020 a quarter of the population will be over 60 (Roberts, 2012, p. 17).

In relation to the United Kingdom as a whole, according to the Department for Innovation, Universities and Skills (2009), by 2030, nearly half the population will be over 50. Ford (2014, pp. 1, 4) records that 'one third of the British population is now over 50. By 2030 the number of people aged over 60 will reach 20 million, according to official figures'. In relation to Northern Ireland, where this book is set, it is estimated that the percentage of people over 85 will have increased by 58% in 2020 (DHSSPS NI, 2011, p. 59).

Cultural commentators on ageing, among them the eloquent Lynne Segal, have offered updates on the rise in the older population, stating that, in Britain, 'ten million people are currently over sixty-five years old, around a sixth of the population, with that number likely to double over the next few decades' (Segal, 2013, p. 2). And older people's organisations have also focused on statistics. According to Paxton (2013, unpaged) there are now 10 million people in Britain today over the age of 65. The voluntary sector organisation, Age NI (2011, p. 5), tells us that there are currently 340,000 older people in Northern Ireland, some 19% of the population.

Looking more broadly towards the European picture, Creighton (2014, pp. 3–4) forecasts that the European population aged over 80 is set to rise significantly. In 1960 just 1.4% of Europeans were over 80. This figure reached 4.1% in 2010 and is projected to increase to 11.5% by 2060. She argues that 'Europe as a whole must adapt to a new world where it is projected that almost 1 in 3 people will be over 65, and more than 1 in 10 will be over the age of 80', adding that the percentage of Europeans aged over 65 is projected to rise from 16.0% in 2010 to 29.3% in 2060.

In the USA, according to Segal (2013, p. 2), 'around forty million people are over sixty-five, some thirteen per cent of the population, with that number predicted to double by 2030, accounting for nearly twenty per cent of the population.'

Demographic change is not just a British or European or US issue; it is an international phenomenon. The World Economic Forum predicts that, globally, the percentage of people aged 60 or over will rise to 22% of the total population in the next four decades, a jump from 800 million to 2 billion (Beard et al., 2011, p. 4). The United Nations Population Fund tells us that one in nine people in the world are now aged 60 or over, with the figure set to rise to one in five by 2050 (United Nations Population Fund, 2012, p. 12).

Responses to the changing demography: the economic and cultural 'construction' of older people

But what is the prevailing attitude to these demographic changes? Despite the United Nations producing a plan of action on ageing in 2002 which recognised the potential of older people in terms of their contribution to society and despite the commitment of Westminster and the devolved assemblies in the UK to ageing strategies (Gray and Dowds, 2010, p. 2), it must be acknowledged that the prospect of a growing older population is almost always presented as a problem or even a crisis; 'doomsday scenarios abound' (Beard et al., 2011, p. 4). This is understandable in one respect; the cost of looking after an expanding section of the population in need of care and support is likely to be considerable. Older people are not infrequently represented or 'constructed' as a burden, as a drain on society, though this is beginning to be challenged (United Nations, 2002; Walker, 2006). The reality is that older people – just like young people – are not a homogenous group, and in the research we conducted and in the literature we consulted, this is strikingly obvious. Many older people do need care in their late years, but so do many young people. All older people are not baby boomers; many live in poverty in the UK and in developing countries (Heslop and Gorman, 2002; Gray and Dowds, 2010, p. 11; Hill, Sutton and Hirsch, 2011). Older people's aspirations and opportunities also vary greatly. And, furthermore, there are vast cultural differences across the globe in terms of how older people are regarded and how they regard themselves. Nonetheless, there is a tendency to lump them all together as a rather homogenous grouping, often in an unjust and ill-informed manner. And there are still too few older people engaged in active learning. As Chen *et al.* (2008) remind us, there is a great deal of work still to be done in gaining the views of those currently not involved in formal education or, indeed, any form of organised learning.

Featherstone and Hepworth (2005, pp. 356–357) point to the pervasive nature of negative or ageist images, citing Warnes's (1993) study of the word 'burden' and its negative association with later life in the popular media and political pronouncements – 'the burden of old age'. Findsen, McCullough and McEwan (2011) also point to the prevalent myths of decrepitude and dependency. Policy documents, such as the Northern Ireland Assembly's Active Ageing strategy (2014), similarly address the issue of stereotyping.

Featherstone and Hepworth (2005, p. 357) echo many other experts in the field of educational gerontology in pointing out that these kinds of negative stereotypes are socially constructed – that is to say, based upon a set of unquestioning attitudes rather than any valid objective evidence. They also cite Gullette's (1997) study of images of older people in fiction, indicating that the most common kind of story about older people is the 'decline' narrative. Segal (2013, p. 263) echoes this. Both fiction and non-fiction 'fix' the social imagination of later life. They refer, in addition, to the work of Hockey and James (1995), who examined the power of images of old age as a process of infantilisation (Featherstone and Hepworth, 2005, p. 357). However, as Segal argues, there are two 'narratives' of ageing: stories or images of progress and stories or images of decline; of ageing well and ageing badly. Segal (2013, p. 18) avers the ageing well narrative can itself be problematic, even contradictory. Segal maintains that the imperative to age well is 'partly complicit with the disparagement of old age' and 'refusing to accept much that ageing entails, including greater dependence, fragility and loss, lines up with the anti-welfare agenda of "neo-liberalism"'. Conversely, she argues, 'those who cannot conceal their need for care are seen as ageing badly.' Some experts, like Hepworth (2000), have examined stories about ageing in terms of how older people are represented, and others, like Tew,

Hubble and Morrison (2012), how older people want to construct their own narratives about ageing.

Featherstone and Hepworth (2005, p. 358) argue that self-esteem arises out of a positive interaction with others who perceive our value. If older people are themselves bombarded with negative attitudes they will, inevitably, experience a diminished sense of their own social worth. And, as we will see in our own research findings, older people can develop a kind of repudiation of any labelling of them as old. Segal (2013, p. 1) plangently notes, 'My very hesitation [in talking about ageing] . . . tells me just how much needs to change before we can face up to the fearful disparagement of old age, including our own prejudices.' There is, she argues, as an older person herself, 'aversion to the very topic of ageing'.

There is, perhaps inevitably, the growth of what might be called the 'Forever Young' industry. Reduce the appearance of wrinkles, get some cosmetic 'enhancement', have a go at the Viagra. It must be admitted that this produces mixed results for older people themselves, but what, we might suspect, continues to look really pretty good is the profit margin of the companies offering such blandishments and, of course, the sales of newspapers and Internet sites crassly guffawing at the 'disasters' arising from older people trying to look like younger people. To be sure, there are also efforts to celebrate the beauty of older people in the fashion and cosmetics worlds, a welcome adjustment, reflecting, if nothing else, the buying power of some older people and the human disposition towards putting our best face out, but also, perhaps, a less cynical engagement with older people. Segal (2013, p. 264) quotes Molly Andrews in her warning that researchers on ageing must resist the temptation of agelessness, suggesting that this denial of difference 'strips the old of their history and leaves them with nothing to offer but a mimicry of their youth'.

Some of the current 'messages' tend to reinforce the notion that it is a very bad thing indeed to be a dependent older person; older people are exhorted to be healthy, to be active. And such campaigns – for they are often presented in this way – are really important, in encouraging older people to 'not fade away', to have faith in themselves and stretch themselves and, of course, relieve the burden on the health and social care services. Segal (2013, p. 262) opines that what everybody hates about the idea of growing older is that it is associated with dependency. 'Yet', she says, 'we do not hear of the "natural" dependency of a child on its parent – somehow older people are not supposed to be dependent', and Segal stresses that the human condition is, in fact, one of interdependence, between people and between generations. In another part of the book Segal (2013, p. 68) cites the anthropologist Barbara Myerhoff, who comments that it is only by maintaining contact with older people that we can come to know ourselves. This will allow us to stop looking at the old 'as an alien remote people unconnected with ourselves'.

Many experts are hopeful, arguing that positive images can be fashioned, that we can reconstruct the negative construction of older people – for example, through calling attention to more images of active retirement (Featherstone and Hepworth, 2005, p. 357). There are also many articles, books and newspaper reports which emphasise the more positive aspects of this changing demography, including the contribution older people themselves can make to sustaining their own wellbeing and contributing to society. Since the late 1960s there has been a gradual growth of books and articles which affirm older people in terms of their capacity, their contribution and the immensely positive benefits they bring to us all. We are regaled in the more thoughtful media outlets with examples of artists, musicians, writers and scientists, still creating into their 80s and 90s. Segal (2013, pp. 65–66, 238–239) includes Verdi, Benjamin Franklin, Frank Lloyd Wright, Michelangelo and Georgia O'Keeffe as well as Rembrandt, Paul Klee, Matisse and Picasso, and Barbara Hepworth includes composers like Bach and Haydn and writers like William Trevor, Alice Munro and Toni Morrison. I might add a few more to this list: Van Morrison, Seamus Heaney, Clint Eastwood, Lili Tomlin and the inimitable Dames Judi Dench and Maggie Smith. Indeed, we would need a whole book to list them all.

What we may note – and bank, to use a contemporary metaphor – is that, in all sorts of ways, some of them a bit contradictory to be sure, the received notions, the hegemony of older people as a burden, as 'other', as 'non-productive' are being challenged. But the people who will contribute most to this challenge are older people themselves. Learning is all about the future. We may learn from the past, its errors, its misconceptions and in relation to attitudes to older people; we can but consider how we can reconstruct, for our own time and for the future, a more innovative outlook for and from older people than their consignment to the status of unproductive burden. Given that older people are mostly portrayed in this way, and thus marginalised, rendered as 'other', it seems to me that it is down to older people to challenge and resist this designation. This is no easy task; as we will see in the responses of older learners in this research project, there is an ambivalence about any labelling of them as old. This reflects what might be described as a kind of internal colonisation, where older people feel obliged to accept the prevailing negative discourse about them and thus to deny that they are older. And yet, in the responses of the older learners, there emerges also a sense that participating in education validates their otherness, offers them a space to be older people.

The 'resistance' to negative 'constructions' of older people began in the very period when the so-called baby boomers were young people. And while this challenge was mounted in other fields – for example, a questioning of the received idea that older people's brains inevitably deteriorate (Welford, 1958) – it is perhaps not significant that one of the pioneers was an educationalist, Howard McClusky. McClusky was, of course, an innovator all his life, but he may be said to be the father of the new field we call educational gerontology. We will hear more from McClusky later in this book; suffice it to say here that in a very straightforward and accessible way, he challenged the prevailing notion that the old dogs could not learn new tricks, arguing that they both could and were keen to learn (McClusky, 1971, p. 416). Sternberg and Grigorenko (2005, pp. 211–212) also argue that 'older people can maintain high levels of performance in some domains by practice, greater effort and the development of new bodies of knowledge'. In another study reported by Sternberg, six components emerged: reasoning ability, sagacity, learning from ideas and environment, judgement, expeditious use of information, and perspicacity.

Education and ageing: can participation in education contribute to the wellbeing of older people?

The context of older people learning: formal and informal modes in lifelong learning and continuing adult education

Our focus in this book is older people in relation to education. And, in recent years, much more attention has been paid by experts in the field of lifelong learning and continuing adult education to the aspirations and rights of older learners (Piley, 1993; Glendenning, 2000; Findsen, 2005; Jarvis, 2010). Many of the experts point to the development of a range of learning organisations, like the University of the Third Age (U3A) and the Elderhostel movement, which focus on informal learning. Some, like Glendenning (2000, pp. 6–7; Sheeran, 2015, p. 37), argue that many older people have turned away from more traditional university provision as not being in tune with what they want to learn and how they want to learn. It is also true to say that university provision for what have been termed 'leisure classes' has also declined. However, there is cause for hope; Dublin City University held its inaugural Age-Friendly Universities Conference this summer, and my report of the work that we have done in Queen's University with older learners found many echoes among the many attendees, most of them older people. We hope to demonstrate that the results of our research within a university setting might challenge the idea that a university cannot provide learning which is in tune with the aspirations and needs of older learners. It will become clear that while our learners testify to the fun and the joy of their learning, they do not regard their learning as leisure, but a serious critical and imaginative engagement with a wide range of subjects, from philosophy to using the Internet for research, to literature to politics to digital arts to languages, from Japanese to Portuguese.

Older people's learning as a new academic field: the rise of educational gerontology

As we will see later in this book, there are now many wonderful experts who have very deeply challenged negative stereotypes of older people within this realm. New disciplines and fields have developed, like educational gerontology, focusing specifically on older people as learners. There is a growing body of evidence to suggest that participation in education does enhance the wellbeing of older people and, indeed, grows and develops their wisdom, their ability to sagaciate. We will look at that evidence when we discuss the findings of the research project. The findings of our research project confirm what the experts say.

Extending wellbeing, wisdom and a process of sagaciation by involving older people as co-researchers

The project has drawn upon many different subject fields in proposing a research project where the students would be involved at every level. That is probably a bit unique, and yet it is a model I have used for many years (Maginess, 2010). Trowler and Trowler (2010, p. 14), for example, complain that, for all the talk of student engagement, students are typically represented as the customers of engagement rather than as the co-authors. Boulton-Lewis and Tam (2012, p. 3) observe that

> there is very little research that describes what older people themselves say they want and need to learn . . . there is no doubt we need more data from older people themselves about their attitudes to learning and why, how and what they want to learn.

The older learners in this project articulated between themselves (for they interviewed each other) not only their honest experience of a particular education programme but also their sagacious recommendations for best practice. They went much further than that, for they talked also about how older people not currently involved in learning could get involved, and what was needed to get them involved. They talked too about how they wanted what they had said to influence policy to encourage more older people to get involved.

But the co-participants in this research also had a lot to say about what it was like to be co-researchers, co-workers. Not one of them said that it was a bad experience. Students, learners, entered and exited that process as they chose; all found the experience to be an agreeable if sometimes challenging process. Some had to learn new skills, some had to revise their own received ideas, while some deepened their understanding of themselves as older learners. Most concluded that they were both learners and sagaciators; that by learning they could question their own ideas and opinions and by having faith in their own their experience and wisdom, they might help the young model the many challenges and doubts and questions they face. Above all, what came across in the responses from older learners was their optimism, their passion for learning and renewal, their resilience in the face of a loss they once thought was very far from inevitable.

The organisation of the book

The first chapter of this book has briefly outlined the action research project which forms the basis of this study and also establishes the broader context in which the study was undertaken – the increasing importance of the age agenda internationally. Changing demography and the cultural construction of older people have been discussed as well as the context of older people's learning and the rise of educational gerontology, and an argument has been made for the benefits not only of engaging older people in education and learning but also of empowering them to be commentators and researchers. The effect of placing older people themselves at the centre of the research process is to further demonstrate their positive potential as authorities and as agents of change.

The next chapter of this book (Chapter 2) offers a much more detailed account of the action research, telling the story of the project. The aim of this is to encourage others – policymakers, educators and older people themselves – to get a concrete, 'lived' sense of how such projects can be done and what lessons may be learned for future co-research projects with older learners. We also wanted to place the specific piece of work we were doing within the wider context of what the experts say about conducting research – that is to say, the methodology of the project – again, hopefully, suggesting some practical as well as theoretical principles which could be considered for future projects. The research paradigm, or model, draws upon many experts across a range of fields, including qualitative research, disability studies, inclusive research, anthropology and educational studies, and the chapter outlines the range of research models that were drawn upon before going on to consider the specific methods and instruments which were chosen and why.

In Chapter 3, the findings of the research in terms of what students had to say about the educational dimensions of their learning are discussed in detail and are related to relevant studies by many experts in the area of educational gerontology. We will discover what motivates the learners, how important the element of choice is for them in determining their own learning pathways and how they view participation as a lifelong journey.

We will then examine what the students had to say about how they are taught and how they learn – what size of classes they like, what styles of teaching they prefer – and we will situate this discussion within theories about pedagogy, andragogy and even geragogy, a new field focusing on teaching and learning with older people. The chapter will also reveal what students consider important in terms of timetabling and assessment before focusing on what makes for enjoyment and wellbeing in their learning.

Chapter 4 focuses on the social dimensions of learning, again situating the findings within a broader policy and academic framework. How participation in an educational programme can enhance social wellbeing is addressed, and we will hear contrasting views from the learners, some of whom consider the social dimension to be relatively unimportant while others value the opportunity for social interaction very highly. In this chapter we will also find out what students had to say about their learning environment, including facilities for students with disabilities, the importance of a welcoming atmosphere and the provision of support materials. What learners had to say about barriers to learning for older people is also recorded.

Chapter 5 focuses mainly on the reflections of the participants in the research. The chapter reveals how older people viewed their experience as researchers. Again, their response is very encouraging, with none reporting that being actively involved in a research project was a negative experience and some very keen to do further projects. Having their views listened to and being able to articulate and voice their opinions were valued greatly by the co-researchers. The opportunity to use their experience and skills they had developed over a lifetime and, equally, to learn new skills was also greatly welcomed and appreciated. And the chance to actively contribute, to be involved in a project that could help other older people, and to the benefit of society, was a salient feature in their reflections.

The final chapter (Chapter 6) offers a number of conclusions and recommendations. The holistic benefits of participation in learning are discussed and situated within the literature from gerontology and educational gerontology. A summary of the key points of the previous chapters will pull together the main lessons to be garnered from the research project. A set of recommendations will be made, based on the findings of our study and on what the many experts in the field have to say. We will address our recommendations to providers, to policymakers and stakeholders and to older people themselves. Our vision is for a much greater investment in older people's learning so that the many claims made for the benefits to wellbeing and wisdom of participation in education and learning can be properly realised for the millions of older people not currently involved in a process that is enjoyable, empowering and life-enhancing, as can be seen in Figures 1.1 and 1.2.

Figure 1.1 Voyages round memory: tutor Carlo Gebler with his class in one of the special courses on ageing.

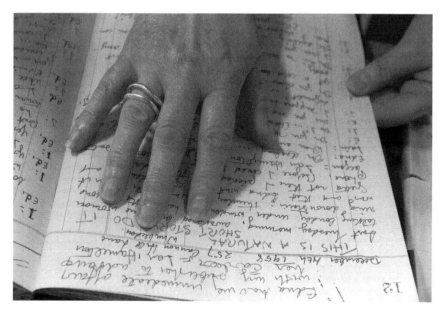

Figure 1.2 Making sense from the past.

References

Age NI. (2011) *Agenda for later life: Priorities for Northern Ireland's ageing society*, Belfast: Age NI.

Beard, J.R., Biggs, S., Bloom, D.E., Fried, L.P., Hogan, P., Kalache, A. and Olshansky, S.J. (eds.) (2011) *Global population ageing: Peril or promise*, Geneva: World Economic Forum.

Beatty, P.T. and Wolf, M.A. (1996) *Connecting with older adults: Educational responses and approaches*, Malabar, FL: Kreiger Press.

Boulton-Lewis, G. and Tam, M. (eds.) (2012) *Active ageing, active learning: Issues and challenges*, New York: Springer.

Chen, L., Kim, Y., Moon, P. and Merriam, S.B. (2008) 'A review and critique of the portrayal of older adult learners in adult education journals, 1980–2006', *Adult Education Quarterly*, 59 (1), pp. 3–21.

Creighton, H. (2014) *Europe's ageing demography ILC-UK 2014 EU factpack*, London: ILC-UK [International Longevity Centre-United Kingdom].

Department for Innovation, Universities and Skills. (2009) *The learning revolution*, London: Department for Innovation, Universities and Skills. Available at https://www.gov.uk/government/uploads/system/uploads/attachment_data/file/228546/7555.pdf (Accessed: 2 February 2015).

DHSSPS NI. (2011) *Transforming your care: A review of health and social care in Northern Ireland*, Belfast: DHSS [Department of Health and Social Services].

Featherstone, M. and Hepworth, M. (2005) 'Images of ageing: Cultural representations of later life', in Johnson, M.L., Bengston, V.L., Coleman, P.G. and Kirkwood, T.B.L. (ed.) *The Cambridge book of age and ageing*, Cambridge: Cambridge University Press, pp. 354–362.

Findsen, B. (2005) *Learning later*, Malabar, FL: Krieger Publishing Company.

Findsen, B., McCullough, S. and McEwan, B. (2011) 'Later life learning for adults in Scotland: Tracking the engagement with and impact of learning for working-class men and women', *International Journal of Lifelong Education*, 30 (4), pp. 527–547.

Ford, R. (2014) 'Over-50 "superboomers" rewrite retirement rules', *The Times*, 4 August, pp. 1, 4.

Glendenning, F. (2000) *Teaching and learning in later life: Theoretical implications*, Aldershot, Hants.: Ashgate Arena.

Gray, A.M. and Dowds, L. (2010) *Attitudes to age and ageing in the North of Ireland*, Belfast, Northern Ireland: ARK [Access, Research, Knowledge].

Hepworth, M. (2000) *Stories of ageing*, Oxford: Oxford University Press.

Heslop, A. and Gorman, M. (2002) 'Chronic poverty and older people in the developing world', CPRC Working Paper No. 10. Available at http://r4d.dfid.gov.uk/pdf/outputs/chronicpoverty_rc/10heslop_gorman.pdf (Accessed: 21 December 2015).

Hiemstra, R. (1992) 'Aging and learning: An agenda for the future', in Tuijnman, A.C. and Van der Kamp, M. (eds.) *Learning across the lifespan: Theories, research, policies*, Oxon: Pergamon Press, pp. 53–70.

Hill, K., Sutton, L. and Hirsch, D. (2011) *Living on a low income in later life*, London: Age UK.

Jarvis, P. (2010) *Adult education and lifelong learning: Theory and practice*, 4th edn, Oxon: Routledge.

Maginess, T. (2010) 'Medium as message: Making an "emancipating" film on mental health and distress', *Educational Action Research*, 18 (4), pp. 497–515.

McClusky, H.Y. (1971) 'The adult as learner', in Seashore, S.E. and McNeill, R.J. (eds.) *Management of the urban crisis*, New York: The Free Press, pp. 27–39 .

Office of the First Minister and Deputy First Minister NI. (2014) *Active ageing strategy: 2014–2020*, Belfast: Office of the First Minister and Deputy First Minister. Available at https://www.ofmdfmni.gov.uk/sites/default/files/consultations/ofmdfm_dev/active-ageing-strategy-2014–2020-consultation.pdf (Accessed: 26 December 2015).

Paxton, J. (2013) 'What older generations can still teach us today' [online]. Available at http://greatbritishcommunity.org/what-older-generations-can-still-teach-us-today/ (Accessed: 27 November 2015).

Piley, C. (1993) 'Adult education, community development and older people', in Edwards, R., Sieminski, S. and Zeldin, D. (eds.), *Adult learners, education and training*, London: Routledge in association with the Open University, pp. 265–276.

Roberts, Y. (2012) *One hundred not out: Resilience and active ageing*, London: The Young Foundation [online]. Available at http://youngfoundation.org/wp-content/uploads/2012/10/100-Not-Out.pdf (Accessed: 27 November 2015).

Segal, L. (2013) *The pleasures and perils of ageing: Out of time*, London and New York: Verso.

Sheeran, Y. (2015) 'Peering into the future', *Third Age Matters*, 16, p. 37.

Sternberg, R. (2005) 'Older but not wiser? The relationship between age and wisdom', *Ageing International*, 30 (1), pp. 5–26.

Sternberg, R.J. and Grigorenko, E.L. (2005) 'Intelligence and wisdom', in Johnson, M. (ed.) *The Cambridge book of age and ageing*, Cambridge: Cambridge University Press, pp. 209–215.

Tew, P., Hubble, N. and Morrison, J. (2012) *Good ageing: The importance of social and cultural narratives; and of older people's continuing control over their personal narratives*. Available at http://www.birmingham.ac.uk/Documents/research/policycommission/AF2120213Tew.pdf (Accessed: 28 November 2015).

United Nations. (2002) *Political declaration and Madrid international plan of action on ageing*, Madrid, Spain: Second World Assembly on Ageing, 8–12 April, New York: United Nations. Available at http://www.un.org/en/events/pastevents/pdfs/Madrid_plan.pdf (Accessed: 27 December 2015).

United Nations Population Fund. (2012) *Ageing in the twenty-first century: A celebration and a challenge*, New York: United Nations population Fund. Available at https://www.unfpa.org/sites/default/files/pub-pdf/Ageing%20report.pdf (Accessed: 27 November 2015).

Walker, A. (2006) 'Extending quality life: Policy prescriptions from the growing older programme', *Journal of Social Policy*, 35 (3), pp. 437–454.

Welford, A.T. (1958) *Ageing and human skills*, London: Oxford University Press.

Withnal, A. and Percy, K. (1994) *Good practice in the education and training of older adults*. Available at http://www.uni-ulm.de/LiLL/5.0/E/5.3/practice.html (Accessed: 13 August 2015).

Chapter 2

Rationale and method
How we carried out the research

Rationale

To conduct a co-research project with older learners about their learning programme offered great potential for connecting an internal enquiry with a topic of pressing relevance well beyond the school and the university, into policy, politics and the community, locally, nationally and globally, and so to contribute to informing a wider discourse. Most especially, our study might be able to challenge the frequently negative stereotyping of older people and also might demonstrate the benefits of participation in education and learning, whether formal or informal, for the wellbeing and wisdom of older people and thus play some small part in prompting policymakers and politicians to consider how access to learning (formal and informal) might be increased and facilitated. Thus, we began in the early months of 2014 to plan for the research by bringing together a steering group.

Setting up the research project

Structure

We were keen that the steering group should have strong representation from among the learners, and we also wanted to gather in expertise from academic areas, like gerontology, cultural studies, adult learning and pedagogy. In addition, we believed that it was important to have voices on the group who represented other groups working with older people, like Age UK (NI) and the University of the Third Age (U3A). We also wanted organisational and strategic thinking skills to help us shape the project. The steering group comprised:

- Two student representatives, one of whom was a former vice-chancellor of the university, and the other who was also a secretary of a local U3A group.
- Six academic experts from gerontology, adult education and learning, cultural studies and pedagogy. Two of these were based in universities in

Scotland and England, to ensure an 'outside' view, and four were drawn from among Queen's staff.

- Four staff from the School of Education. Two were tutors in the Open Learning Programme and co-directors of the programme (one of them myself), and the other two were invited because of their expertise in qualitative research and intergenerational work (one a Health Visitor researcher, the other with a social science background).

In retrospect, we perhaps should have had more student representatives, and based on how the project unfolded, where the potential of students as active researchers was so fully realised, as well as ensuring a better balance, I would recommend a higher proportion of students on the steering group for other such projects. Nonetheless, I would say that the student representatives not only made valuable contributions to the steering group but also engaged as interviewers and interviewees, so they punched well above their numbers.

Funding

How was the project going to be financed? The default position in response to such a question is almost invariably to apply for funding. I had received a National Teaching Fellowship in 2013 and the money was burning a hole in my pocket. In truth, I had a number of ideas about how to spend it, but very often the best ideas come from other people, so I began to think that this enquiry would be a good way of honouring the great faith put in me by the Higher Education Academy, as it allowed for a kind of research that was very much rooted in how we taught and how we learned and what belief systems and support systems we had to centre our students. We did apply for a grant but the funder, experiencing cutbacks, was not able to consider it. While a larger grant would have enabled us to employ professional researchers, in the end, we were able to manage. I looked carefully at the generous £10,000 National Teaching Fellowship award, and, having worked in voluntary and community organisations, had figured that we could, with careful husbandry, cover the costs of expenses for students involved in the research project, the costs of steering group members attending three or four meetings and the bringing in of expertise from other departments in the university to help us with promotion and the filming of the special courses.

A two-stage project

We agreed to conduct the research in two stages; the first stage would involve setting up a series of 'interventions' – that is to say, a pilot project which could test how older learners responded to 'special courses' on the topic of ageing, which would be evaluated. Tutors would also be interviewed to obtain their views. The second stage would be a more general co-research project where older learners would interview other older learners about their experience of the Open Learning Programme, including their attitude to the special courses.

What would the research 'produce'? Outputs

The next question we had to ask ourselves was what sort of tangible products could we produce through this research – what would its 'outputs' be? We came up with the following 'projected outputs':

- *A series of special courses focused on the topic of ageing*, which would be evaluated to determine whether learners wanted to engage with issues on ageing, and if they did, what kinds of subjects or approaches might be most congenial and empowering for learners.
- *A book* which would share what we all had learned from our own reflections on the Open Learning Programme, and which would also draw on the relevant 'literature' – what experts in education and ageing were saying about older people and learning in terms of their capacity to learn, their motivations (or lack of) for learning, their access to learning, their participation or lack of it, what kinds of contexts they learned in, what styles of learning were best suited and what kinds of support structures and environments were most conducive. Thus, we were keen, from the outset, to see how we might connect our particular experience with what the experts were saying (or as the experts would say, 'contextualise' our particular project), so that we could gain a broader perspective, apply some of the current theories to our own Open Learning Programme and also, in a modest way, contribute our insights, the wisdom of our learners, to these broader academic and policy debates.
- *Two independently peer-reviewed articles*: I was keen, from the outset, that students, if they wished, should be actively involved in making these articles. And that is a bit unusual, because nearly all articles tend to be produced by academics.
- *A project website*. The idea was to share what we were learning, as we were learning it, with other older people involved in education, formal or informal, with older people's organisations, regionally, nationally and internationally, with relevant policymakers and with centres of ageing and educational gerontology, internationally.

Promoting the project – including documenting and evaluating from the start

Given that we were keen to inform our learners about the project as soon as possible, so that we could get them involved, letting them know the general aims and purposes and also about the special 'intervention' courses, we engaged with the university's media services and produced an information leaflet to be distributed across as many classes as possible, well in advance of the spring programme. In retrospect, I am not sure that the leaflet completely translated my very detailed brief that we create an image of older people learning that was surprising and at the same time familiar and reassuring. I think we got across the 'reassuring' message better than the 'surprising' message, and I should have spent more time with the designers. On the other hand, the original image from the designers was so psychedelic that even the most colour-hardened survivors of the 60s among our older learners might have been a bit blinded by the bright. In the end, 250 copies of the leaflet were printed and distributed across a range of classes. Tutors also spoke to students about the project and we uploaded the leaflet onto our Open Learning Programme website (see Figure 2.1).

Research ethos and research models

Research ethos

The steering group offered much sound advice and expertise, especially in relation to the ethos of the research and also about the choice of research models or paradigms. As stated in the introduction, the ethos of this research project is about trying to learn from our learners about how to make our particular programme better and, beyond that, how to encourage more older people to participate in education and also about challenging negative stereotypes of older people and fostering a change in society whereby older people are valued for the positive contribution they are more than capable of making to society. In short, education and research should be about trying to make society better, to affect change. And this is often done by giving voice to those whose voices are often drowned or ignored, who have been cast as marginal or 'other'. Evidence-based research – that is, research based upon the expertise of those who understand what it is like to be viewed as marginal – can tell an important tale. And that tale is often based upon strategies of resistance and resilience. The 'othered' voices can teach us all about humour and optimism and sagacity and can become agents of social transformation (Freire, 1970, rpt. 1993; Habermas, 1984; Carr,1995; Torres, 1996). Contingently, the research ethos centres on older learners as the makers of research. The deeper purpose of co-research is fundamentally about striving for greater democracy, equality and social justice. So, I would follow educational theorists like Finlay (2002), Hunt (2009) and Ellis, Adams and Bochner (2011), who say that creating a vehicle for *voicing* is a way of empowering the silent, those who are not generally asked for their views. As Finlay (2002, p. 211) argues, the purpose of such 'co-constructed' research is to 'reframe power balances between participants and researchers'.

Figure 2.1 Promotional leaflet for Sagaciation: enhancing the wellbeing and wisdom of learners.

Special Open Learning Spring courses examining attitudes to older people

We plan to run a special series of courses in the Spring Programme focusing on age.

Creative Writing: Voyages Round Memory
Carlo Gebler, 5 weeks, Tuesdays, 11am-1pm, staring 6 May

Schooldays: The Best Years of your Life?
Cathal McManus, half-day workshop,
Wednesday 14 May, 1pm-4pm, Folk and Transport Museum, Cultra

**Representations of Older People in Culture:
Tattered Coat or Purple Coat**
Tess Maginess, 5 weeks, Thursdays, 2pm-4pm, starting 8 May

Life History project: From Object to Memory to History
Clodagh Brennan Harvey, 5 weeks, Tuesdays, 7pm-9pm, starting 6 May

'Pass Me the Jam': Ageing Postively
Aideen Gildea, 2 weeks,
Wednesday 14 May, Wednesday 21 May. 10.am-1pm

To enrol, visit our website at www.qub.ac.uk/edu/ol, or request a copy of our brochure.
From 7th April, you can also enrol by telephone: 028 9097 3323

We gratefully acknowledge the support of The Institute for Collaborative Research in the Humanities

A study to discover whether participation in Open Learning enhances the wellbeing of older people

We will then conduct a study with older learners to find out whether participation in the special courses and other Open Learning courses enhances the wellbeing of older people. We plan to interview between 30 and 50 people, individually or in focus groups. We will look at factors like cost, support, teaching and learning styles and location. The study will involve getting your views through interviews and focus groups about the special courses we are running in the spring programme and, more generally, about the Open Learning programme. We are keen to learn from you how we can improve the programme.

We know from our experience that older people are often 'sages' and have a huge amount to contribute. We will draw on your sagacity, the wisdom you give us, to make a special manual, showing others how to develop first rate education projects with older people. There will also be a project website which you can contribute to. We warmly welcome your participation.

How can you participate?

You can enrol for one of the special courses and let us know your views, before and after. You can also get involved with us in conducting the study, for example as an interviewer (we will provide training), by contributing to the project website (which will create an international forum for older learners) or practice manual (the 'how to' book, made by you, as learners, demonstrating how older people can articulate their ideas about what the very best open learning programme would be like), or by helping to document the project, eg through photography or video or writing.

Please feel free to contact Tess Maginess, who will be leading the project, if you would like any further information before making your decision. Email: t.maginess@qub.ac.uk   Telephone: 028 9097 2512
In writing: School of Education, Queen's University, 20 College Green, Belfast, BT7 ILN

If you would like to get involved, please give us your contact details:

Name _____

Address _____

_____

Telephone number _____

Email address _____

Figure 2.1 (Continued)

Research models or paradigms

Since this book is aimed at many different kinds of readership, including people who are not academics, the aim is not really to engage in an extended academic debate about research models and approaches, about which a huge number of books and articles have been written, but rather to set the research project we embarked upon into a broad theoretical context and thus to offer a rationale for how we did the research and why. The academic experts on the topic of how to do research distinguish between two basic 'paradigms' or models: quantitative and qualitative (Cohen, Manion and Morrison, 2005; Neuman, 2005; Booth, Colomb and Williams, 2008; Creswell, 2014). In the quantitative model, which is still the predominant model, researchers are mainly concerned with volume and numbers. So, for example, clinical trials of a new drug to treat cancer might demonstrate that this drug is more effective for many more people or researchers can demonstrate that climate change is occurring at a certain rate. In this book we saw examples of quantitative research earlier when various statistics were quoted in relation to changing demography. Qualitative research is more concerned with how people respond if the demography is changing, how it affects their view of themselves and their place in the world.

The study we were embarked upon was from the outset envisaged as qualitative rather than quantitative. We could have followed a quantitative model and distributed a survey to our 6,000 students, but the detailed analysis of this would have required a much larger budget. There is no doubt that a larger-scale quantitative study could have furnished us with important data, and it is to be hoped that such a study might be possible in the future, encompassing not just our Open Learning Programme but also others. Ideally, a mixed methods study, incorporating both quantitative and qualitative models, would have furnished a greater range of data.

This research project was also conceived of as involving students/learners in as many ways as possible, or to put it another way, challenging the traditional model, where the academic expert interviews the research 'subjects'. For this reason also, a qualitative approach, which would involve a small-scale, in-depth process of discovering the quality of the students' experience, seemed a good fit in the circumstances.

Qualitative research: involving the 'subject'

Traditionally, experts, usually academics, have tended to see themselves as the authoritative voice and the people interviewed as 'subjects'. But there has been some serious questioning of this in what has been termed by academics, across a number of subjects, 'the reflective turn' (Mascia-Lees, Sharpe and Ballerino Cohen, 1989; Schon, 1991; Foley, 2002; Tanaka, 2002; Mauthner and Doucet, 2003). We see, for example, the evolution of user and emancipatory research in disability studies, the emergence of 'inclusive research' and 'participative research' within qualitative research and, in the education field, the growing pre-eminence of 'constructivist' approaches, which foreground the importance of learners as active, reflective and even as co-producers of learning and, indeed, research – most especially approaches like critical pedagogy, deriving from Freire (1970), constructionism deriving from Piaget (1972) and constructivism (Wertsch, 1998) and communal constructivism (Holmes *et al.*,

2001). And, as Messiou (2014) argues, engaging with students' voices is in itself a manifestation of being inclusive.

It is not my intention here to offer a wide-ranging discussion of the huge topic of the history and reach of each of these terms, but simply to give a flavour of the context and meaning of each, so that it will become clear why they have been chosen for this particular project.

User-based research

These newer terms – and behind the terms, these new approaches – have come from a wide range of fields. I have encountered, for example, the term 'user-based research' in work I have been involved with in the field of disability studies (Oliver, 1997; Lynch, 1999; Barnes, 2001; Tew, 2003; Walcraft, Read and Sweeney, 2003; Rose, 2004; Russo, 2012). User-based research has emanated, as the name would suggest, from 'users' of 'services' – often people with a disability and their carers. And the impetus for this approach has been, to put the matter very plainly, a creative and empowering response to the dissatisfaction often experienced by service users and carers with the 'system', with stereotypes and negative attitudes towards disability and with a lack of respect towards their expertise and their voice. So, they started to develop their own kind of research, where their knowledge, insight and expertise could be articulated.

It seems to me that there are some clear parallels between the situation of disabled people and carers and that of older people. We must be very careful not to view people with a disability or older people as a homogenous group, and it will become clear in the research findings that there are many shades of opinion and even directly contradictory viewpoints among older people. And our participants represent only a small cross section of older people.

While there has been a huge expansion in the literature about ageing and older people, all too often we still see older people represented in the popular media as an undifferentiated group, and furthermore, as a negatively stereo-typed 'group'. Splendid work has been done by academics and some older people themselves, but we are still not hearing nearly enough 'user voices' when it comes to older people. And while, as I have indicated in the intro-duction, the once tiny field of educational gerontology has now expanded like St Bridget's cloak, into a very substantial and fertile stead, the involve-ment of older students as researchers is still something of an untilled pasture, despite the calls of theorists like Habermas that the voice of all concerned should be heard (Rushton and Suter, 2012, p. 98).

The central purpose of this book is to foreground the differentiated voices of older people, and their advocates – to paraphrase Seamus Heaney's poem, 'Miracle', they 'who were with them all along' (Heaney, 2010, p. 17) in every aspect of the research about them. The students in this study are the 'users' of a particular educational 'service', but they had much to say beyond the particular programme. And they were keen that their voice, their views, might help to make things better for other older people who currently do not participate in lifelong learning and to contribute to their society. This vision of education stretches back as far as Aristotle and is echoed in the 1930s by Dewey, and later in the century by theorists like Paulo Freire. Later experts like Carr were part of another new field called 'critical educational science', and this is based on the postulation that education should be a critique of society and that action research should, consequently, lead towards political and social change (Rushton and Suter, 2012, p. 98).

This particular project lays no claims to do anything other than raise the potential for 'user-focused' participative research. Such an approach could, in a very modest way, signal some directions for how older people could become empowered and empower others to change their attitudes and strengthen the argument for increased access to forms of learning and education which value the insights and wisdom of older people. It is hoped that projects like this might demonstrate how older people can challenge the pernicious and disastrously myopic hegemony of their representation and thus, in a small way, act as a catalyst for change.

Action research and educational action research

Action research aims to undertake an investigation with the goal of changing and improving the situation of the participants and bringing about change in their own environment or even in society. Much has been written about this approach (Somekh, 2006; Eikeland, 2007; Reason and Bradbury, 2013). Within the specific context of teaching, 'action research' is now commonly deployed as a model through which teachers can develop 'reflective practice' – that is to say, a way of working which encourages the teacher, as well as the student, to operate within a kind of virtuous cycle of reflecting and questioning what they are doing and why and how, trying new 'interventions', evaluating these and then improving practice as a result (Cohen, Manion and Morrison, 2005).

Central to action research is the deployment of what is called a learning cycle. This suggests that people engaged in real learning go through a continual cycle of reflecting on experience, attempting new ideas or gaining new knowledge, reflecting and evaluating on that and drawing out the wider lessons. David Kolb (1984) was the inventor of this concept and his very influential book places great emphasis on the importance of the experience of the learner. This is especially relevant to our project, since older learners brought not only a wealth of experience from a range of different fields but also several years' experience of participating in adult education and learning upon which they could reflect.

Participatory research and co-research

Participatory research or evaluation is another, related, model which has been used in education. Cousins and Earl (1995, p. 4) draw upon applied social research and management theory when they refer to the importance of professionalising teachers by encouraging 'enquiry mindedness'. Granted, that is a slightly cumbersome way of expressing the simple enough proposition that teachers should be self-critical, that they should, as we used to say, 'examine their conscience' in terms of whether they are teaching well. And how are they to be guided as to what constitutes good or bad teaching? There are two ways; they can read what all the theorists say and or they can listen to their own students, or both. The beauty of adult education is that neither students nor teachers are constrained by national curricula or league tables or any of the other frameworks which can open up fissures between what must be taught to test and what can be taught to enrich knowledge and skill in a subject. Cousins and Earl are in line with current thinking about organisations as 'learning entities', and this project, in its own small way, has the aim of teaching the teachers and all those involved in the support of students how we can learn to improve our own programme by listening to our learners, our 'clients', our customers. The control, say Cousins and Earl (1995, p. 9), should not be centred on the researcher, a sentiment with which we heartily concur.

From the outset we were keen to involve learners in all aspects of the research, building on previous projects in which students had been actively involved. In addition to participating in the steering group, students would be invited to contribute in a range of ways: as interviewers and interviewees, as creative documenters (using photography or illustration) through blogs or diaries or film-making, as data analysts, as organisers, as researchers of the literature on the subject, as writers, editors and website contributors. We wanted to encourage learners to be active co-researchers and co-creators of the project, using as wide a variety of 'entry points' as possible, drawing, on the one hand, upon skills they already had from their previous life and thus valuing the huge range of expertise among the learners, but also encouraging the learners to try their hand at new skills and knowledge. This means actively involving the subjects in the research. Ledwith (1997, p. 73) cites Opie's term (1992) 'co-research'. The whole idea is to give greater value to the voices of participants (Grbich, 2007, p. 13).

Co-research takes participatory research a step further; the traditional 'subject' works alongside the academic researcher, and is involved in all aspects of the research project. This approach is now more widely adopted across different research fields, from community work to tourism to psychology to education (Hartley and Benington, 2000; Epston, 2004; Rushton and Suter, 2012; Mura, 2015). As Finlay (2002, p. 211) argues, the purpose of such 'co-constructed' research is to 'reframe power balances between participants and researchers'.

In this project, we wanted to build on previous learning projects to activate a co-research model that would, as it were, work from top to toe, or to put it another way, the principle of students/learners being involved in all aspects of the research process, from initial design to final writing up. So, from the outset, we envisaged students/ learners being involved and influencing the whole project. Logically, this evolved from a regular process whereby the students evaluated the courses in the Open Learning Programme every year. The evaluations were very carefully and meticulously scrutinised both internally and by an external moderator. Recommendations coming from students were communicated to tutors and monitored. Students could also express delight or dismay formatively, and so, for example, if we were receiving 'feedback' that a particular course was not quite as well organised as it should have been, or that the tutor was not communicating effectively, we would act on that straight away.

In addition, with my own courses, I had developed a practice of encouraging students to shape the syllabus – in literature courses, the writers and subjects they suggested were incorporated. In courses with smaller numbers there is also an opportunity to have open sessions in which they present on writers or books they were especially fond of or share their own creative pieces. And the teaching and learning styles are consciously participative, enabling learners to contribute actively to discussion. I will have more to say about this in the next chapter, when the findings of the research will be discussed.

Over the years I have been involved in a number of education-in-the-community projects in which the model of co-research was worked out in practice in a very rich and complex manner. Many of these projects were with what are termed 'non-traditional learners' and also disadvantaged communities, defined geographically or demographically or in terms of communities of interest – for example, around disability or gender. Many of the participants were suspicious of a university; most were sceptical that adult education could offer them any experience that was not characterised by irrelevant learning, remote and often harsh teachers and a total insouciance about their own knowledge and expertise. But when the learning project had relevance to them and when they were free to shape it and when the learning and teaching styles were not traditional, with the teacher being always in the governing position of expert and unquestioned authority, they began, slowly, to connect with it (Maginess, 2011).

Developing an intergenerational dimension: involving the 'young ones' as co-researchers

Early on in the project I had already sought to develop links with other colleagues in the university who were working on other projects with older people, including the ARK project. Through colleagues, especially in the social sciences, three young master's students came forward to help. Of the three, one was unable to commit, but the other two joined us. For these students, the project represented an opportunity not only to engage in an intergenerational project but also to hone their skills as researchers. At a later stage in the project, another master's student from the School of Education joined the team, working primarily on the expert literature in the field of educational gerontology. Thus, a project like this offers potential not just for sharing knowledge and understanding between older and younger learners, but also as a platform for enabling young researchers to gain 'hands-on' experience. The young researchers gave generously to the project and had important skills to share with us also. We will hear more about how they got on when we reflect on the research process in a later chapter (Chapter 6).

Insider research and auto-ethnographic research

In some of these projects I was also an insider researcher; that is to say that I shared the experience of being a carer and, in relation to this project, I share the experience of being an older person and in working with the Open Learners over many years. I worked alongside the learners as a researcher. Such an approach has its advantages and disadvantages. The main advantages are that, because trust has already been built with the participants, there is a foundation for 'rapid and complete acceptance by participants' (Gray, 1980; Noddings, 1995; Corbin Dwyer and Buckle, 2009, p. 58) and the expertise of the researcher and the participants can be shared, thus enhancing the depth and breadth of knowledge. The project draws upon values like trust and warmth, building on relationships we have established over many years with our students. One disadvantage may be that there is bias or a lack of objectivity (Kanuha, 2000; Rooney, 2005; Boudah, 2011, p. 145; Unluer, 2012). Another may be that those interviewed will tell the academic researcher what they want to hear. Anthropologists like Peter Metcalf (2002) and educational researchers like Peter Clough (1999) have laconically testified to this experience. Some of the newer, so-called auto-ethnographic research, in which the researcher comments about his or her role in the process, can run aground on the endlessly shifting sands of an endless examination of conscience in which, once again, the academic can become the real focus, and his or her 'meta-commentary' on the *process* of the research for the researcher may paradoxically erase the very 'subjects' he or she is so keen to cherish. The 'subject' drifts away, swims home. However, at its most focused, the auto-ethnographic approach and the acknowledgement that research can be 'messy' may fail to deliver all that the academic researcher wants it to (Finlay, 2002; Cook, 2009; Maginess, 2010; Quicke, 2010). Nonetheless, this research approach can yield rich results. Coghlan and Cagney (2013, p. 4) recommend that researchers pay heed to the 'embedded knowledge' which comes from the direct experience of the participants.

But, of course, I was also an outsider, to some extent, in that I was, in a certain way, in charge of the research and indeed the training of the co-researchers, so it could be said that I occupied the position of a 'border-crosser', moving between the situation of being an insider and being an outsider. Flick (2004, p. 112) characterises the position that I occupied as that of the 'initiant'. I think this is a reasonable representation of the situation. My position in the research was to be both an insider and an outsider, a co-researcher laying no claim to any authority in the research and open to criticism also as a co-director of the programme.

Research methods and instruments

We decided that we would use the following instruments:

- Course evaluations.
- Interviews (students and tutors).
- A literature review.
- A questionnaire to co-researchers.
- Creative, arts-based documentations.

Why so many instruments? Triangulation

Leading academics in the field of qualitative research emphasise the advisability of 'triangulating' results by using more than one mode for gathering 'data' (Denzin, 2001; Golafshani, 2003; Flick, 2004; Boudah, 2011, p. 78). Though academics take this very specific use of the term for granted, it is not immediately obvious to non-academics what it might mean. Some of us may remember triangulation from geography or mathematics – you figured out what point you wanted to get to by measuring the distance from known points and, by making a triangle, figured out the not-known point. In social science and education research, the same basic principle applies. If only one method or mode of collecting information or 'data' was used, the researchers might rightly face the charge that the findings were not reliable or not valid. So, for example, by using only interviews, the potentially known points of the evaluations would never become evident. The data (the point, if you will) cannot be said to be reliable or valid or in the right place, because you are measuring it from only one side. Triangulation not only allows researchers to fill gaps that might be left by using just one method, but also, more importantly, adds to the richness of the material collected, including the possibility that the answers, the points, as it were, might be different, depending upon the research instruments used, what sorts of questions are asked, how they are asked and of whom they are asked.

At any rate, it is arguable that we could have used more research methods and indeed, more modes. However, not all the methods we suggested in the leaflet about the project for getting involved were taken up. As we noted in the previous chapter, while learners who met with me signalled a desire to become involved and often gave the most articulate and poignant private testimonies, a few did not, in the end, wish to make these available. Nobody submitted a poem or a critical commentary or an email or a blog; only two or three people wanted to get involved in training to film the project and nobody composed a song or a funny sketch. In retrospect, perhaps we should have done more to persuade learners to participate in these ways.

Research questions

The next stage was to try to articulate a research question and a set of subsidiary questions. After some thought, and after discussing the idea with very helpful colleagues, I came up with this formulation of the research question: 'Does participation in the Open Learning Programme (as an example of a formal adult education programme) enhance the wellbeing and wisdom of older learners?'

The sub-questions were:

- What are the main advantages for older people of engaging in the Open Learning Programme?
- Why do students enrol?
- What do students think of the courses in terms of content/subject matter?
- Should there be special courses focused on ageing? (Do older learners see themselves as older learners or just learners?)
- What do they think of the learning and teaching styles?
- Have students acquired new skills and knowledge or just consolidated what they knew already? Has a process of sagaciation, wisdom making, taken place?
- Have students made any friends or developed social networks? (Does participation help to combat isolation and the marginalisation of older people?)
- What do students think of the support systems (front-of-house, disability services)?
- Are there barriers to participation?
- What would students like to change about the programme that would enhance their wellbeing?
- Is it good value for money, affordable?
- Does participation in the programme contribute to wellbeing, wisdom and sagaciation?

(A full list of the interview questions is contained in Appendix 3.)

Implementing stage 1: the 'interventions': special courses on ageing

While it may not be a truth universally acknowledged that a good action research project must be in 'want' of an 'intervention', we came to believe that a specific intervention would deepen the study and really get older learners thinking in relation to issues for themselves around ageing. In our case, the most logical form of 'intervention' was a suite of special courses on ageing. We mulled over this and we were keen to approach the topic from a whole variety of perspectives, partly to enable students to perceive the many-sided facets and many subject categories under which the topic of 'ageing' was relevant and partly to encourage them to approach ageing from a perspective that was relevant and meaningful for them. The leaflet (whatever its limitations) was distributed during the 2014 winter term to give students enough time to enrol in the special courses which were due to take place in the spring term, after Easter, and/or indicate that they wanted to be involved in the research project in other ways.

We decided to offer a mix of tried and tested subject areas, together with newer subjects, and equally, in terms of tutors, we decided to offer a suite of courses which featured some well-known and popular tutors, to create a greater sense of familiarity, and a couple of new tutors, to challenge the students and to ascertain if ageing as a topic was, in itself, appealing. The proposed 'intervention', to be encompassed within the Open Learning spring programme of 2014, was the following courses:

1 *Lifelong Learning: New Tricks.* The course was to be designed in conjunction with Age UK with a group of older learners not engaged with the Open Learning Programme. The course was to be facilitated by Dr Tess Maginess with input, where appropriate, from facilitators from the other practice interventions and other experts. The curriculum themes, content and mode of delivery would be determined by older people.

2 *Storytelling: 'I Could Write a Book'.* To be facilitated by Clodagh Brennan-Harvey, an international expert on storytelling, this five-week workshop series would enable older people to critically examine stories about older people and to tell/write their own stories, charting their memories of their own youth, and to bear witness to their current life.

3 *Creative Writing: Voyages Round Memory.* This five-week workshop series would enable students to directly engage with acclaimed writer and teacher Carlo Gebler, as he charted a way through his 'work in progress', based upon the archive of writings produced by his father as he descended into dementia. The students would be encouraged to consider a range of issues around memory and memory loss, the function and role of writing in relation to the production of narrative, fabulation and contradictory stories/voicing, as well as working with Carlo on creative questions about form, genre, characterisation and structure.

4 *Representations of Older People in Culture: Tattered Coat or Purpled Coat?* To be facilitated by project team member Tess Maginess, this five-week workshop series would focus on the range of representations of older people in literature, the visual arts, the performing arts and film (e.g. Shakespeare, Yeats, Dylan Thomas, Jenny Joseph, Swift, *Amour,*

The Marigold Hotel, Hosseini, Heaney, Rembrandt). The aim of the workshop series would be to empower students to challenge negative media representations of older people, discover the diversity of representation of age across the arts and construct their own creative images.

5   *Healthy Ageing: Pass Me the Jam*. This would be facilitated by Aideen Gildea, health visitor/researcher, who was involved in the early stages of the project, and peer tutors; this short workshop course (two mornings) would examine current imperatives for healthy ageing and empower participants to offer their own views about this mantra. The idea would be to cast a slight irreverent and questioning light upon the much bruited importance of healthy ageing and to solicit from learners what they felt constituted wellbeing and good health. Perhaps, it might turn out that a little of what you fancy might do you good, even though it might be just slightly unhealthy, like jam.

6   *Intergenerational Perspectives on Age: Cycling Life*. To be facilitated by Laura Dunne, a psychologist, who was involved in the early stages of the project, this short workshop (two mornings) would bring together a group of young students with older students to examine intergenerational views of older people around themes of interaction, engagement and connectedness. Drawing upon examples of intergenerational practice and personal perspectives, older students would reflect on how, when they were young, older people were regarded by society and what they now think about being older and how they are regarded, and young students will critically reflect on their own views of ageing. Older people would thus act as peer tutors, revealing the resources and wisdom that come with age. Issues of wellbeing will be central, especially in terms of how generations can connect and support each other.

7   *Schooldays, the Best Days of Your Life?* To be facilitated by project team member and Open Learning Programme academic Cathal McManus, this short workshop course (one morning), conducted in a reconstructed schoolroom at the Ulster Folk and Transport Museum, Cultra, some 20 miles from Belfast, would stimulate learners to compare their own experiences of their schooldays with how and why they were learning now as older adults.

As might be expected, not everything worked out according to plan. It transpired that one of the tutors fell ill, another was required to focus on other professional imperatives and the proposed collaboration with Age UK (NI) did not materialise, due to pressure of work on their staff.

Students as peer tutors

In one of the courses, 'Healthy Ageing: Pass Me the Jam', I was able to persuade two students on literature courses who had been medical doctors in a previous life to contribute their expertise to their fellow learners as peer tutors. I met with them to discuss the brief in detail and they were both very enthusiastic, committed and organised. I was able to offer some mentoring about how they might shape their medical expertise within a workshop setting. This is a way of involving students which has much potential, and I will return to this in the final chapter. There is no doubt that students as peer tutors can form another way of empowering learning and enabling them, as Qureshi (2012) argues, to participate in learning as a social practice.

Other forms of participation: using creative approaches in documenting the special courses

Arts-based or creative approaches to documentation and research are becoming more popular within the qualitative paradigm (Knowles and Cole, 2008; Leavy, 2008; Finley, 2011). Just as being an interviewer was one mode of enquiry, or working on the literature review was another mode, so too students were encouraged to contribute to the range of research modes by drawing upon their own skills in areas like illustration, photography and creative writing. But why would we want to do this? After all, the research output of the book, for example, would be perfectly fine without photographs of participants taken by a student. Well, I suppose I am of the generation which is apt to say, 'waste not, want not.' More seriously, inviting students to bring creative skills into the project was not just another way of making the study more fully participative, in a way that was organic, drawing on the expertise of the learners; it was also our aim to make our 'learning products' or, if you will, research results more accessible, more aesthetically pleasing. The reader might thus be brought into closer contact with the students who made the research and would also be presented not with stock images of older people but original, real images of them in their own learning environment.

Filming

Early on in the project I had also engaged in discussions with our audio-visual unit in the university. It was my original intention to offer students training in recording and filming interviews. As it transpired, the take-up for this was very small, so instead I worked with the unit, which filmed sessions from all of the courses.

Planning for the scheduling of the filming took quite a bit of time as the courses were all in different locations and at different times. We began with a sort of 'recce', to figure out in advance what issues might arise in relation to the different locations. Some of the rooms were, for example, quite small, so the crew had to think ahead in terms of where they might position themselves. We did consider moving some of the classes for the filming, but concluded that this would be too disruptive for the students; we did not want the tail to wag the dog. As it transpired, the variety of locations did contribute a richness and texture to the filming. Three of the four courses were filmed in different classrooms on campus and the fourth 'on location' in a reconstructed schoolroom from the early part of the twentieth century which is part of our Folk and Transport Museum in Cultra, County Down. Permissions were negotiated with the staff of the museum. This proved fairly straightforward as Cathal McManus, who conducted the special course 'Schooldays, the Best Days of Your Life?', had already held Open Learning courses at Cultra as part of our outreach programme. Members of the museum staff were most helpful and gracious. Students were happy to travel from Belfast as there is a very good rail connection and the course represented a pleasant 'outing', with nobody really complaining about having to squeeze into the old-fashioned 'forms' or bench desks. Indeed, the 'scholars' behaved themselves in an exemplary fashion, resisting the temptation to squirt ink or 'cog' each other's homework.

Consent forms for filming and the taking of stills had been incorporated in the ethics proposal, and these were distributed to students in advance, so that there were no horrible surprises, nor a rush for 'selfies' – fame at last. We arranged that the filming for the longer courses be done after a week or two so that the students and tutor would be into their stride. In the case of the two short courses, this was not possible. One student did not wish to be filmed, and the crew handled this most sensitively so that she was not identifiable. Indeed, the cameraman and sound man carried out their work very unobtrusively and stayed for at least two hours so that they were able to get a real feel of the classes. The students very quickly relaxed during the filming. The crew had plenty of material to edit and I was invited to a viewing of the 'rough cut'. Miraculously, they had managed to condense several hours of filming down to about 30 minutes and had cleverly intercut tutor interviews with shots from the classes themselves.

Photography and illustration

Before the special courses ran, I approached one student who had expressed an interest in becoming involved and asked her if, as a professional photographer, she would be willing to bring her creative skills to bear in documenting the project. This student, Jane McComb, gave very generously of her time, attending sessions for all the special courses and photographing both students and tutors. Jane worked alongside the film crew, and this proved to be a very efficient way of carrying out the documenting, since the students were not 'subjected' to more than one round of visual scrutiny. Somewhat later, I discovered that another student, Charles Brannigan, who had been an architect, was also keen on illustration. The illustrations in this book are his contribution.

The project website

It was our original intention to 'upload' film and stills onto the website. Regrettably, while good progress was made on designing the content and format of the website, pressure of time has not, at this stage, allowed us to proceed beyond this. Again, it is a feature of the real life of any action research and co-research project that not everything that is initially hoped for ends up happening. It is to be hoped that we will be able to revive the idea at a later stage.

Stage 1: course evaluations and interviews with tutors

Evaluations were conducted among the students enrolled in the special courses (Appendix 1) and tutor interviews carried out (Appendix 2). These were filmed. I acted as interviewer for all except my own course, where Cathal McManus took on this role. The results will be reported in the next chapters.

Course evaluations are perhaps the most immediate way of gauging learners' views. Our evaluations are distributed physically at the end of each new course, and the advantage is that this tends to produce a high rate of response. Poor response is a problem for many mainstream evaluation systems, as Stark and Freishtat have argued (2014, p. 4). Smith and Morris (undated) also confirm that response rates can be low, partly due to the fact that students are inundated with survey requests. Many of our learners come back each year to continue their journey of learning for more courses. So they are familiar with completing course evaluations as these are distributed on a regular basis and always for new courses. They are then, arguably, unlike most undergraduates, more expert in evaluation (Stark and Freishtat, 2014, p. 7) and because all the courses are 'elective' rather than prescribed or mandatory, they are more inclined to offer honest and well-informed comments. Gravestock and Gregor-Greenleaf (2008) conclude that course evaluations are generally reliable, though there are unclear concepts and definitions of effective teaching and debate about the use to which evaluations are put by institutions.

It must be acknowledged that course evaluations can really only offer a snapshot of students' views about teaching, organisation, accessibility of tutors and so on. This is one of the reasons why we also carried out tutor evaluations and also conducted qualitative interviews with students.

Stage 2: co-researching the Open Learning Programme

Thirty or so people indicated that they would like to be involved as interviewees or interviewers; others expressed a wish to be involved but were not quite sure how. I conducted a number of one-to-one meetings with these learners and from this exercise I drew up a task list, identifying all the different kinds of work in which students could get involved. I provisionally allocated names, according to what area learners had told me they would most like to contribute. The main tasks were identified as follows:

Organisation

- Setting up database of all interested 'contacts'.
- Setting up an electronic and manual filing system to ensure that proper records were kept of all aspects of the project, including consent forms for interviewing, filming and photography, transcripts of interviews, literature review material, course materials from the special courses, student evaluations, project documentation.
- Timetabling and scheduling interviews.

As it turned out, we had one student who had a background in computers and had worked for the Civil Service, who set up an excellent database with all project contacts incorporated, drawing upon information received from the 'tear-off' slip on the leaflets. Another student, with lots of experience in training and interviewing, furnished a template for scheduling interviews. It is clear already that learners not only drew upon the skills, experience and wisdom they already had but also met the challenge of using this experiential learning to embark on a new kind of project.

Conducting research

- Submission of ethics proposal to the School Ethics Committee.
- Training in interviewing, conducting a literature review and data analysis.
- Participating in interviews.
- Reading and analysing material for the literature review.
- Data analysis (from evaluations, interviews, questionnaires encompassing insights from the literature review).
- Conducting a questionnaire among the co-researchers.
- Writing/editing.

Ethics submission

The research proposal was submitted to the Ethics Committee of the university and was approved with minor amendments. We had familiarised ourselves with the 'best practice' guidelines produced by the British Educational Research Association (2011), the gold standard for research in the field of education, and were especially keen to give respect and value to the learners as co-researchers, not as 'subjects' for academic research.

Training of student researchers

Interviewers

There is in academic circles, understandably, a strong emphasis on 'professional' research, carried out by professional researchers. Yet, as we have seen, some of the academic literature espouses the importance of 'learner voices', user-based, participatory co-research. Our view was that, within a small-scale project, it would not be possible or even necessary to train researchers to what we might term postgraduate standard. Nonetheless, we were fully aware that the project could not be taken seriously if we just fired our learners into interviews with no guidance and no input from them. It would also be ethically very suspect.

While the cohort of older learners in this project were perhaps somewhat accustomed to 'voicing', even to taking part in interviews or, perhaps more commonly, market surveys, and interviewing people in their work in the past, the business of being interviewed and of interviewing is, unless you are a politician or a journalist, still a rather uncommon and artificial experience for most of us. In considering the training of interviewers, we were keen to collapse as much as possible the boundaries between interviewer and interviewee and to have a high regard for the generosity of both parties, interviewer and interviewee, in entering upon this curious, slightly surreal relationship.

So who was involved in the training, what did we 'cover' in the training and how did we cover it? As it happened, through the self-selection process, some people were willing to be interviewed and also to be interviewers. I suppose, for some this might seem a curious and even questionable state of affairs, but to me that seemed a deluxe state of affairs, because it would create a sort of double whammy – those participants who were both interviewees and interviewers would gain a kind of dual perspective. So, having been 'subjected' to being an interviewee, they would have a more critically reflective attitude about what they would do differently if they were an interviewer. And the gap between interviewer and interviewee would be, as a consequence, narrower and more nuanced.

We organised two workshop sessions as not all those who were interested in being interviewers could attend the first workshop. Again, the importance of being flexible and of organising the training to meet the lives of the student researchers seemed to us an important principle in terms of genuine co-research. In other words, it is not all about the academics and their schedule. In the sessions, we covered ethics, the questions to be asked, interview techniques, modes of recording, venues and expenses.

The ethics section was fairly straightforward; there was general agreement and understanding around not harrying interviewees, about respecting any confidential personal information given, about respecting the time limits and about assuring interviewees that they would, unless they waived the claim, be anonymous, that they could withdraw from the process at any time and that data would be securely stored.

Participants were presented with the draft interview questions and offered some minor revisions which we incorporated. In terms of interview techniques, the importance of putting interviewees at their ease as much as possible was emphasised. Interviewers were reassured that if interviewees strayed 'off mission' in terms of answers to specific questions, this was fine and that it was also fine for the interviewer to comment, to 'disclose' their own experience, as long as this did not overwhelm the dialogue with a 'wait till I tell you' monologue from the interviewer. Jokes occurred.

When it came to how interviewers would 'collect the data', participants were left free to choose how they wanted to record the interviews; some found the availability of a digital recorder helpful, a much less intrusive piece of 'kit', compared with the old, invasive 'reel to reel', while others preferred to take notes and others elected to use both methods (Weiss, 1994). It should be noted that, given the particular age spectrum of the cohort, most over 50 were accustomed to extensive note taking rather than digital recording, so in the actual interviews, this method was generally deployed. However, the younger researchers felt more comfortable with using digital recording with notes as a backup.

The training sessions were, relatively speaking, quite short as it was a small-scale project. Nonetheless, the much more sustained training offered in the programmes outlined in a Joseph Rowntree–sponsored participant research project involving older people in the UK is to be much admired (Clough *et al.*, 2006), though it must be said that this project was rather more complex than ours. In the case of our project, the training was set up in direct response to the aspects of the research that the learners themselves identified. We were also very conscious that students were volunteering their time and we did not wish to place an undue burden upon their goodwill.

As a follow-on from the training, to ensure that participants were as confident as possible, the opportunity to do a practice or pilot interview under my supervision was also offered and three or four of the participants subsequently took up this offer. Feedback was given and interviewers affirmed that this was useful to them, enabling them to refine their technique and also to be a bit more relaxed and conversational.

Some of the interviewers word-processed the handwritten notes they had taken, and that was an additional charge upon their time. Not all were in a position to do that, and it should also be noted that one of the young researchers very kindly typed up handwritten interview transcripts. That was a great help as it was a pretty time-consuming process.

Training in data analysis

Two student researchers were involved in this, one a young master's student and the other an Open Learning Programme student. I offered informal training to each, individually, especially on 'thematic analysis' of the data – that is to say, what the experts call 'immersion' in the data, or, put more simply, looking at answers repeatedly and sifting what is relevant (Miles and Huberman, 1994; Pope, Ziebland and Mays, 2000), to determine recurring themes emerging across different interview responses and across different interview questions. Two students working on the same data with myself enabled triangulation of results.

Training in conducting a literature review

Initially, one student from the Open Learning Programme, Allen Young, professed an interest in co-researching the literature review. I conducted informal training with this student and then arranged for him to have further specialised training from our subject librarian in sourcing relevant databases. In the summer of 2015 master's student Asma Niazi joined us. As she was familiar with how to conduct searches and with academic writing and referencing, she received individual training on the scope of the literature review.

Collecting the data

Interviews with students by students

Byrne (2012, p. 209) argues that qualitative, semi-structured interviews are especially appropriate when attitudes and values are to be explored, especially 'voices which have been ignored, misrepresented or suppressed'. And, as Wengraf (2001) states, the semi-structured interview is a joint production between the interviewer and the interviewee.

In addition, we reckoned that a set of face-to-face interviews would enable the learners to be much more at ease and to have the sense that their opinions and experience were being valued and paid attention to. Mason (2002, p. 62) calls for a relatively informal style when conducting semi-structured or qualitative interviews, citing Burgess (1984), who categorizes these kinds of interviews as 'conversations with a purpose'.

As Flick (2004, p. 123) argues, interviewers should be people with the necessary knowledge, experience and capability to reflect on the subject. The sample framework was 'purposive', in that those who came forward all had the advance knowledge needed (Wilmot, 2005, p. 4). Of course, there are arguments against this: we might run the risk of hearing only the most extreme views, or the more shy might not want to be interviewed, even though they might have some great things to say.

As noted earlier, some 250 information leaflets were distributed across a range of classes, some tutors spoke to students, encouraging them to take part in the project in whatever way they wished, and the leaflet was also posted on the Open Learning Programme website. While the larger 'sampling frame' (Seale, 2011, p. 138) was some 6,000 students, it was recognised that, given that this was a qualitative study, relying on interviews as the principal method of data collection, the response would likely be small; we calculated that if 20–30 students agreed to be interviewees and/or interviewers, that was a realistic and meaningful sample. For us what was important was depth, as Flick (2004, p. 124) expresses it, to 'further penetrate the field'.

Some 26 students agreed to be interviewees and/or interviewers, and a total of 24 interviews were carried out by eight interviewers, some of whom were also interviewees. Wilmot (2005, pp. 3–4) is of the view that for this kind of study a sample of between 20 and 50 is appropriate as the purpose of the research is not to produce a 'statistically representative sample'.

In terms of gender breakdown, 8 of the interviewees were men and 16 were women. Of the interviewers, all but one were women. The higher number of women would be reflective of the pattern in the Open Learning Programme and, indeed, more generally, in formal continuing education programmes (Findsen, 2005, p. 73). While we did not attempt to establish the socio-economic profile of the participants on the ground that in a qualitative study of this kind, where the request for such information may well have seemed intrusive, my knowledge of the students would indicate that most of them came from professional backgrounds and were well educated. Again, this would tend to be typical of formal education programmes involving older people (Glendenning, 2000, pp. 6, 22; Findsen, 2005, p. 72). All participants were White; again this would be fairly typical of the demographic of older people in Northern Ireland and the population statistics of the Northern Ireland Statistics Agency (2013, pp. 1–2) confirm this. As Percy (1990, p. 43) puts it, 'Females, middle-class people and well educated people are more likely to participate than males, working class and those with no educational qualifications.'

During May 2014, we drew up a schedule of interviews. I made contact with all those who had indicated that they were willing to be interviewed and confirmed their permission to be interviewed. This was to ensure that interviewees had an 'opt out' if it no longer suited them to take part and also to request permission to be contacted directly by the interviewer to make arrangements that would suit both parties for the interviews to take place. We agreed that we would conduct the interviews across the summer to allow plenty of time for holidays and other commitments. It may be noted that some of the interviewers were also interviewees, so these participants gained a kind of double perspective. We agreed that each interviewer would take on no more than three interviews. This was to make sure that the burden was not excessive and that we would have a good variety of interviewers. The interviewees and interviewers were matched on a purely random basis and were coded to ensure anonymity. I also conducted four interviews. As noted earlier, we did three 'pilot' interviews, all of which I observed, and participants received constructive feedback.

Interviewers either typed up the transcripts and sent or delivered them to me, where they were kept in a locked drawer or, in a couple of cases, submitted handwritten notes, which were kindly typed up by one of the young researchers. Interviewees were also given an opportunity to read the transcript and add or alter anything they wished. This was to ensure that participants were satisfied with what had been recorded and also to give a further opportunity to interviewees to make additional comments. With great help from the co-researchers, the interviews were complete by early September 2014.

Most were held in rooms I had booked in our own school or in my office. The building would be well known to our students, and we deliberately chose small, informal rooms to create a more relaxed atmosphere. Interviewers and interviewees were given the choice of conducting their interviews in other locations, if this proved to be mutually convenient. The only stipulations we made were that the space was accessible (since some of our older learners have mobility problems), was culturally neutral (an important factor in Northern Ireland, where some venues are considered to be identified as 'Catholic' or 'Protestant') and was quiet and comfortable (there is nothing less conducive to getting people talking than a freezing room or one which is overheated or has only hard chairs) and that the interview could not be overheard by others (assuring confidentiality).

Interview questions

As Maxwell (2013, p. 77) argues, 'research questions identify the things you want to understand . . . your interview questions generate the data that you need to understand these things.' The questions were designed to link with the research questions but were more disaggregated – that is to say, we broke down the various sub-research questions into greater detail. In addition, we were conscious that interviewees might find an initial 'open question' less intimidating and we also returned to the issue of wellbeing in the final question so that the interviewees, having gained a bit of confidence and, so to speak, warmed to their subject, might provide a more expansive answer. This proved, indeed, to be the case. That some of the questions could have been better framed, or were interpreted in different ways, we have no doubt and we will discuss these issues in the next chapters, reporting on and analysing the findings of the research. The interview questions are listed in Appendix 3.

Literature review

I also spent quite a few immensely happy hours over the spring and summer working on what is known in academia as a literature review. Most research projects, whether in the academic world or beyond it, incorporate a literature review. When I first encountered this term, many years ago, I have to say I was surprised and delighted because for me it implied that scholars thought that reading novels and poems and plays were important for understanding any subject. That turned out not to be what is understood by the term. Rather, a literature review is, as I understand it now, a critical analysis of the (mostly) academic writing about the subject to be studied. By late autumn of 2014, I had amassed a fairly substantial literature review, annotating what I had read and organising it into the broad sections indicated earlier. Co-researcher Allen Young spent countless hours reading many books and articles, some of them an extension of his own former professional expertise as an occupational psychologist, but many well beyond the call of his former calling. Asma Niazi, a master's student in the School of Education, later joined the team to assist with the literature review and also made a very important contribution.

The reason for doing a literature review is that researchers can place their particular study within the many-mansioned house of other studies and theories. One undoubted benefit is that a particular study does not stand all alone and rather frail but derives authority from an understanding of what all sorts of experts have previously said about the subject, especially what Cohen (1977) and Usher and Edwards (1994) call international leading edge theory.

Finding out what the leading edge theories are is, itself, a learning process; the researcher is not trying to assert that she or he knows it all, but rather can receive valuable guidance from those who have gone before, even though the project has its own original character. And the literature review is a way of paying tribute to the scholars who have already written in the field.

In conducting a literature review, it was important to think first about the scope of it. What we had in mind was not an exhaustive inventory and analysis of all the 'literature' produced by academics and policymakers about ageing, or even about older people and learning/education, or even about older people as researchers, but rather, a more selective analysis.

Changing demography and perceptions about ageing

Given that the project was inspired partly by an apprehension that the topic of ageing was becoming ever more important due to the global demography indicating an expanding population of older people, I believed it was important to check out the facts on this, so that we had an 'evidence-based' approach. So facts and figures from both academic research and government policy documents about ageing populations would be important, as well as paying some attention to the huge expansion of literature about ageing – for example, in the field of gerontology.

I also believed it was important to take a look at how older people were perceived and how they perceived themselves. There is a huge amount of work now in this area, across a number of disciplines and beyond that into more popular 'literature'. Sometimes the term 'cultural construction' is used by academics. Just as societies 'construct' disability, they also come up with certain 'images' about older people and about the prospect of ageing, some of them still very negative.

Older people and adult learning/education: educational gerontology

Zoning in a bit from these very big issues, I wanted to focus on what the experts had to say about older learners more specifically, since our project was, after all, to do with education. Educational gerontology is a growing field, so a study of articles emanating from this area was important. Also important were books and papers from the world of adult education and lifelong learning.

Older people as researchers, students as researchers and older students as researchers

I also wanted to look specifically at any literature that looked at older people being actively engaged in research in any subject area, then to look at students who were involved in co-research and finally at research on older learners co-researching about their learning.

Data analysis

After the interviews were concluded, I conducted a preliminary analysis of the data, or to put this more plainly, I read through all the evaluations, interview transcripts and questionnaires, as well as revisiting the film footage and photographs, and formed an initial impression of what our students were telling us and showing us. Allen Young, one of our Open Learning Programme students and one of the young researchers, also volunteered to do some basic data analysis on the interviews. The data analysis would also, of course, have to draw upon the literature review in some way, so that we could compare our results with what the academic experts had to say about older people and learning.

Co-researcher questionnaires: 'meta-commentary'

In the initial research design of the project, I had not really considered any form of 'follow-on' questionnaire to those who had participated. I suppose I had not realised myself quite how considerable the breadth and depth of engagement from the students would be. Nor did I fully understand what the process of being involved, especially as researchers, would really mean to them – and to me. Contingently, in terms of how I saw the 'research product', I did not foresee that the process of the research was to become so central. I am reminded, ruefully, of a response attributed to the novelist E. M. Forster, when asked by an interviewer what his next book was going to be 'about'; he replied with another question: 'how do I know what I am going to write about until I have written it?' And while we do not intend to smother the project with endlessly auto-critical or auto-ethnographic introspection, there is a certain persuasive logic for researchers in an action research project to reflect also on the process of the research, not just its findings and to provide a 'meta-commentary', their views about being involved as co-researchers.

In this case, the 'instrument', a questionnaire, was chosen because I did not wish to impose too much upon those who had already very generously given their time and enthusiasm and skills, new and not so new. And, because there were, in the end, quite a long list of people who had, in a variety of ways, actively participated, it would have been difficult to schedule another set of interviews or arrange focus groups. The questionnaire was designed to encourage participants to comment on the specifics of their experience as active participants. A list of the questions can be seen in Appendix 4.

Given the emerging importance of the *process* of being involved as active participants in the study in a range of modes, I made the decision to 'capture' as part of the data the views of all those who were involved in terms of what they thought of being involved – did their active engagement in actually evaluating and commenting upon and documenting and peer teaching and organising and researching and writing contribute to their wellbeing and wisdom? Researchers and/or participants commenting on the process of the research is known as meta-commentary or meta-research. The views and voices of the participants about their experience as co-researchers are vital as a means of informing us about whether older people want to be actively involved in research about topics relevant to themselves and how, exactly, they want to be involved.

Making a book

Having studied the various forms of data, we then pulled out the main findings – what we were being told by our learners about their experience of the courses, including the special courses, and, more broadly, what their experience of being involved in a formal education programme was like and how it might be improved to enhance and valorise their wellbeing and wisdom – and compared these with what we had found out through the literature review. We will discuss these findings in the following chapters.

In the light of what has been said before about the emerging importance of the involvement of learners themselves in the study, as co-researchers, enacting wellbeing, wisdom and sagaciation at a deeper and more dynamic level, we then analysed the data from the participant questionnaire, augmenting this with the literature review. Learners embraced the challenge of also being researchers and documenters, and this became a salient dynamic of the research process. The results will be reported in Chapter 6.

Our last task was to try to pull the study together by offering a set of conclusions and recommendations, addressed not, as is so often the case, to mid-air, but to what are called 'stakeholders' – they who have a voice and are capable of exerting influence on policy, politics and even cultural 'conditioning'. It is to be hoped that the voices of learners will sing to all who read this book.

Limitations of the study

Every study, inevitably, will have limitations. As noted earlier, it would have been delightful to have had the funding to conduct both quantitative and qualitative research. Had funding been available, we would probably have deployed two or three academic researchers, but the principle of having students as researchers would have remained central to the project ethos. Whether better data and a better analysis of the data could have been produced by professional researchers is more open to debate. With more academic research expertise available we could certainly have carried out a somewhat larger study, and that may have revealed a more complex data picture or stronger backing for common responses. This is a small-scale study and we acknowledge that, while we have tried to connect our data with other studies and academic studies on older people's learning, not all of our findings or recommendations will be 'transferable'. We hope, however, that many of them will be.

With more academic research expertise available, we might also have offered more sustained training – though there is an argument that students would not have committed to this. We will analyse the researchers' own responses in a later chapter. A further limitation may have been that, as students self-selected to become involved, it may have been that the cohort over-represented students who knew me. There are two aspects to this – the data we collected may have been too strongly representative of students studying humanities subjects, especially literature. However, it must also be said that at least half the students involved were not, by profession, English teachers or even history teachers; we had, for example, doctors, occupational psychologists, a librarian, a dental nurse, an engineer, a professional trainer, an economics professor and a couple of civil servants. In relation to the students knowing me, it could be argued that this was an efficient way of recruiting participants – better the devil you know. Again the answers given in the participant questionnaire will address this point.

Another limitation of the study, which I have drawn attention to earlier, was that, while we did have representation of the project's steering group from a voluntary organisation working with older people, Age UK (NI), we did not succeed in gaining traction for a special course (taster workshops), despite Age UK (NI) being very enthusiastic about this. As a result, we were not able to collect data about the experience of older people who might not be involved in formal adult education or, indeed, informal education. It would have been very useful to compare 'in the field', though we did analyse many books and articles about older people's learning – formal and informal – in the literature review and will reflect this in the findings chapter.

There are many other limitations: none of us had ever done a study like this before, we were all greenhorns, *ingénues*, and we were learning on the job. It was all a bit experimental, a bit high-risk. But, I have to say, that was also, time and time again, part of the privilege of being involved; nobody – least of all myself – knew what exactly we were searching for, never mind how to find it. That we fetched up at a different place from where we started there is no doubt. And, to me, that is a valid state of affairs, for if we simply researched questions to which we already knew the answers, we would never learn anything worth knowing. The greatest discovery of this project has not been how older people can skilfully, critically, creatively enact a new way of being as active voices, but that they are so rarely *asked* to meaningfully engage, on their own terms. And what a loss that is. Despite the very many limitations of this study, for which I take responsibility, I think the potential that, in its small way, evidences, voices or illustrates is to be ignored at all our peril, for what older learners have taught us is exciting, dynamic, supple, wry, compassionate, provocative, tolerant and, dare I say, most valuable of all in our stressed-out, anxious and unfunny world, a dear-bought, deep humour, as can be seen in Figures 2.2 and 2.3.

Figure 2.2 Best days of your life: tutor Cathal McManus, with his students in a reconstructed classroom from days gone by at the Folk and Transport Museum, Cultra, Co. Down, attempts to impose a little discipline on the unruly returning scholars.

Figure 2.3 Open Learning Programme student June Smart (RIP) egging on her fellow scholar, Joan Semple, to make a little mischief in the schoolroom.

References

Barnes, C. (2001) '"Emancipatory" disability research: Project or process?' [online]. Available at http://disability-studies.leeds.ac.uk/files/library/Barnes-glasgow-lecture. pdf (Accessed: 3 December 2014).

Booth, W.C., Colomb, G.G. and Williams, J.M. (2008) *The craft of research*, 2nd edn, Chicago and London: The University of Chicago Press.

Boudah, D.J. (2011) *Conducting educational research: Guide to completing a major project*, London: SAGE.

British Educational Research Association. (2011) *Ethical guidelines for educational research*, London: British Educational Research Association.

Byrne, B. (2012) 'Qualitative interviewing', in Seale, C. (ed.) *Researching society and culture*, 3rd edn, London: SAGE, pp. 207–226.

Carr, W. (1995) *For education: Towards critical educational inquiry*, Buckingham: Open University Press.

Clough, P. (1999) 'Crises of schooling and the "crisis of representation": The story of Rob', *Qualitative Inquiry*, 7 (3), pp. 428–448.

Clough, R., Green, B., Hawkes, B., Raymond, G. and Bright, L. (2006) *Older people as researchers evaluating a participative project*, York: Joseph Rowntree Foundation [PDF]. Available at http://citeseerx.ist.psu.edu/viewdoc/download?doi=10.1.1.504.1511&rep=rep1&type=pdf (Accessed: 3 April 2015).

Coghlan, D. and Cagney, G.A. (2013) '"Multisensory holistic immersion": The method of insider inquiry skills as a threshold concept', *Journal of Learning Development in Higher Education*, 5, pp. 1–20 [online]. Available at http://www.aldinhe.ac.uk/ojs/index.php?journal=jldhe&page=article&op=view&path%5B%5D=136&path%5B%5D=135 (Accessed: 15 August 2014).

Cohen, L. (1977) *Educational research in classrooms and schools: A manual of materials and methods*, London: Harper and Row.

Cohen, L., Manion, L. and Morrison, K. (2005) *Research methods in education*, 5th edn, London and New York: RoutledgeFalmer.

Cook, T. (2009) 'The purpose of mess in action research: Building rigour through a messy turn', *Educational Action Research*, 17 (2), pp. 277–291.

Corbin Dwyer, S. and Buckle, J.L. (2009) 'The space between: On being an insider-outsider in qualitative research', *International Journal of Qualitative Methods*, 8 (1), pp. 54–63.

Cousins, J.B. and Earl, L.M. (eds.) (1995) *Participatory evaluation in education: Studies in evaluation use and organizational learning*, London: The Falmer Press.

Creswell, J.W. (2014) *Research design: Quantitative, qualitative and mixed methods approaches*, London: SAGE.

Denzin, N.K. (2001) *Interpretive interactionism*, 2nd edn, London: SAGE.

Eikeland, O. (2007) 'Why should mainstream social researchers be interested in action research?', *International Journal of Action Research*, 3 (1+2), pp. 38–64.

Epston, D. (2004) 'Narrative therapy and research', *International Journal of Narrative Therapy and Community Work*, 2, pp. 31–36.

Findsen, B. (2005) *Learning later*, Malabar, FL: Krieger Publishing Company.

Finlay, L. (2002) 'Negotiating the swamp: The opportunity and challenge of reflexivity in research practice', *Qualitative Research*, 2 (2), pp. 209–230.

Finley, S. (2011) 'Critical arts-based inquiry', in Denzin, N.K. and Lincoln, Y.S. (eds.) *The SAGE handbook of qualitative research*, 4th edn, London: SAGE, pp. 435–450.

Flick, U. (2004) 'Triangulation in qualitative research', in Flick, U., von Kardoff, E. and Steinke, L. (eds.), Jenner, B. trans., *A companion to qualitative research*, London: SAGE, pp. 178–183.

Foley, D. (2002) 'Critical ethnography: The reflexive turn', *International Journal of Qualitative Studies in Education*, 15 (4), pp. 469–490.

Freire, P. (1970; rpt. 1993) *Pedagogy of the oppressed*, London: Penguin Books.

Glendenning, F. (2000) *Teaching and learning in later life*, Aldershot, Hants.: Ashgate Publishing Ltd.

Golafshani, N. (2003) 'Understanding reliability and validity in qualitative research', *The Qualitative Report*, 8 (4), pp. 597–606.

Gravestock, P. and Gregor-Greenleaf, E. (2008) *Student course evaluations: Research models and trends*, Toronto: The Higher Education Quality Council of Ontario.

Gray, R.J. (1980) 'How do you teach the elders?', in Glendenning, F. (ed.) *Outreach education and the elders: Theory and practice*, Stoke on Trent: Beth Johnson Foundation Publications and Department of Adult Education, University of Keele, pp. 31–44.

Grbich, C. (2007) *Qualitative data analysis*, London: SAGE.

Habermas, J. (1984) *The theory of communication in action. Vol 1: Reason and the rationalization of society*, McCarthy, T. trans., Boston: Beacon Press.

Hartley, J. and Benington, J. (2000) 'Co-research: A new methodology for new times', *European Journal of Work and Organizational Psychology*, 9 (4), pp. 463–476.

Heaney, S. (2010) 'Miracle', in *Human chain*, London: Faber and Faber, p. 17.

Holmes, B., Tangney, B., FitzGibbon, A., Savage, T. and Meehan, S. (2001) 'Communal constructivism: Students constructing learning for as well as with others', in *Proceedings of the 12th International Conference of the Society for Information Technology & Teacher Education (SITE)*, Charlottesville, VA, pp. 3114–3119. Available at www.editlib.org/j/SITE/v/2001/n/1/ (Accessed: 24 March 2016).

Hunt, C. (2009) '"They pass by themselves without wondering": Using the self in, and as, research', in *Really useful research: Critical perspectives on evidence-based policy and practice in lifelong learning. SCUTREA annual conference proceedings* [online]. Available at http://www.leeds.ac.uk/educol/documents/181937.pdf (Accessed: 15 July 2015).

Kanuha, V.K. (2000) 'Being native versus "going native": Conducting social work research as an insider', *Social Work*, 45 (5), pp. 439–447.

Knowles, J.G. and Cole, A.L. (2008) *Handbook of the arts in qualitative research: Perspectives, methodologies, examples and issues*, London: SAGE.

Kolb, D. (1984) *Experiential learning: Experience as the source of learning and development*, Englewood Cliffs, NJ: Prentice Hall.

Leavy, P. (2008) *Method meets art: Arts-based research practice*, London, NY: The Guilford Press.

Ledwith, M. (1997) *Community development: A critical approach*, Birmingham: The Policy Press.

Lynch, K. (1999) 'Equality studies, the academy and the role of research in emancipatory social change', *The Economic and Social Review*, 30 (1), pp. 41–69.

Maginess, T. (2010) 'Medium as message: Making an "emancipating" film on mental health and distress', *Educational Action Research*, 18 (4), pp. 497–515.

Maginess, T. (2011) 'Paradoxes unbounded: Practising community making', *European Journal for Research on the Education and Learning of Adults*, 2 (2), pp. 209–225.

Mascia-Lees, F.E., Sharpe, P. and Ballerino Cohen, C. (1989) 'The post-modernist turn in anthropology: Cautions from a feminist perspective', *Signs*, 15 (1), pp. 7–33.

Mason, J. (2002) *Qualitative researching*, 2nd edn, London: SAGE.

Mauthner, N.S. and Doucet, A. (2003) 'Reflexive accounts and accounts of reflexivity in qualitative data analysis', *Sociology*, 37 (3), pp. 413–431.

Maxwell, J.A. (2013) *Qualitative research design: An interactive approach*, 3rd edn, London: SAGE.

Messiou, K. (2014) *Responding to diversity by engaging with students' voices: A strategy for teacher development*, Southampton: University of Southampton.

Metcalf, P. (2002) *They lie, we lie: Getting on with anthropology*, Oxon: Routledge.

Miles, M.B. and Huberman, A.M. (1994) *Qualitative data analysis: An expanded sourcebook*, London: SAGE.

Mura, P. (2015) '"To participate or not to participate?" A reflective account', *Current Issues in Tourism*, 18 (1), pp. 83–98.

Neuman, W.L. (2005) *Social research methods: Quantitative and qualitative approaches*, 6th edn, Boston: Allyn & Bacon.

Noddings, N. (1995) 'A morally defensible mission for schools in the 21st century', *The Phi Delta Kappan*, 76 (5), pp. 365–368.

Northern Ireland Statistics Agency. (2013) 'Census 2011: Detailed characteristics for Northern Ireland on ethnicity, country of birth and language', *Statistics Bulletin*, Belfast: Northern Ireland Statistics Agency.

Oliver, M. (1997) 'Emancipatory research: Realistic goal or impossible dream?', in Barnes, C. and Mercer, G. (eds.) *Doing Disability Research*, Leeds: The Disability Press, pp. 15–31.

Percy, K. (1990) 'Opinions, facts and hypotheses: Older adults and participation in learning activities in the United Kingdom', in Glendenning, F. and Percy, K. (eds.) *Ageing, education and society: Readings in educational gerontology*, Keele, Staffordshire: Association for Educational Gerontology, pp. 24–46.

Piaget, J. (1972) *The psychology of the child*, New York: Basic Books.

Pope, C., Ziebland, S. and Mays, N. (2000) 'Qualitative research in health care: Analysing qualitative data', *BMJ*, 320 (7227), pp. 114–116.

Quicke, J. (2010) 'Narrative strategies in educational research: Reflections on critical autoethnography', *Educational Action Research*, 18 (2), pp. 239–254.

Qureshi, M.A. (2012) 'Group dynamics and peer tutoring: A pedagogical tool for learning in higher education', *International Education Studies*, 5 (2), pp. 118–124.

Reason, P. and Bradbury, H. (eds.) (2013) *The SAGE handbook of action research: Participative inquiry and practice*, 2nd edn, London: SAGE.

Rooney, P. (2005) 'Researching from the inside – does it compromise validity?-A discussion', *Level3*, 3, unpaged [online]. Available at http://level3.dit.ie/html/issue3_list.html (Accessed: 3 March 2014).

Rose, D. (2004) 'Telling different stories: User involvement in mental health research', *Research Policy and Planning*, 22 (2), pp. 23–30.

Rushton, I. and Suter, M. (2012) *Reflective practice for teaching in lifelong learning*, Berks.: Open University Press.

Russo, J. (2012) 'Survivor-controlled research: A new foundation for thinking about psychiatry and mental health', *Forum: Qualitative Social Research*, 13 (1), Art. 8, unpaged.

Schon, D. (1991) *The reflective turn: Case studies in and on educational practice*, New York: Teachers' College Press, Columbia University.

Seale, C. (2011) 'Sampling', in Seale, C. (ed.) *Researching society and culture*, London: SAGE, pp. 134–152.

Smith, P. and Morris, O. (undated) *Effective course evaluation: The future for quality and standards in higher education*, London: Electric paper Ltd [online]. Available at http://www.lse.ac.uk/newsAndMedia/aroundLSE/archives/2011/effective EvaluationReport.pdf (Accessed: 4 December 2015).

Somekh, B. (2006) *Action research: A methodology for change and development*, Maidenhead: Open University Press.

Stark, P. and Freishtat, R. (2014) 'An evaluation of course evaluations', *Science Open*, pp. 1–26 [PDF]. Available at http://www.stat.berkeley.edu/~stark/Preprints/evaluations14.pdf (Accessed: 4 December 2015).

Tanaka, G. (2002) 'Higher education's self-reflexive turn: Toward an intercultural theory of student development', *Journal of Higher Education*, 73 (2), pp. 263–296.

Tew, J. (2003) 'Emancipatory research in mental health', *Social Perspectives Network for Modern Mental Health, Paper 4* [PDF]. Available at http://spn.org.uk/wp-content/uploads/2015/02/SPN_Paper_4.pdf (Accessed: 4 February 2014).

Torres, C.A. (1996) 'Adult education and instrumental rationality: A critique', *International Journal of Educational Development*, 16 (2), pp. 195–206.

Unluer, S. (2012) 'Being an insider researcher while conducting case study research', *The Qualitative Report*, 17, pp. 1–14.

Usher, R. and Edwards, R. (1994) *Postmodernism and education*, Oxford: Routledge.

Walcraft, J., Read, J. and Sweeney, A. (2003) *On Our Own Terms*, London: Sainsbury Centre for Mental Health.

Weiss, R. (1994) *Learning from strangers: The art and method of qualitative interview studies*, London: The Free Press, Simon & Schuster.

Wengraf, T. (2001) *Qualitative research interviewing*, London: SAGE.

Wertsch, J.V. (1998) *Mind as action*, New York: Oxford University Press.

Wilmot, A. (2005) *Designing sampling strategies for qualitative social research: With particular reference to the Office for National Statistics Qualitative Respondent Register*, London: National Office for Statistics [online]. Available at http://wwwn.cdc.gov/qbank/QUest/2005/Paper23.pdf (Accessed: 12 March 2014).

Chapter 3

Findings

The educational dimensions of older people's learning

What we discovered from older learners about their experience of the Open Learning Programme

The responses from learners fell into three basic areas: the educational dimensions of older people's learning, the social dimension and the learning environment and dimension, and the broader impact of participation on health, wellbeing and wisdom. This chapter deals with the educational aspects, discussing and analysing the key findings of the co-research.

Course evaluation comments (Appendix 1) and responses to the tutor questionnaire about the special courses (Appendix 2) have been incorporated as augmentation to the interview questions (Appendix 3) and to create 'triangulation' – or a range of views of the topic. In relation to the interviews, respondents often supplied multifaceted answers. We have also peppered this account with direct quotes from the learners, the better to enable their voices to be central. What follows is a thematic analysis of the data, grouped around what emerged as recurring factors students identified as contributing to their wellbeing, placed within the context of relevant literature.

Educational dimensions of older people's learning

The chance to pursue individual learning pathways

A large number of responses indicated that what learners liked best was the availability of subjects or topics which appealed to their particular interests. This is very much in line with what Knowles (1984) identified as the self-directed nature of adult learning. One learner said that she felt the ability to choose among a wide range of topics was very 'empowering'. The academic experts express this as students being enabled to pursue their own individual learning pathways. Glendenning (1995, p. 154), for example, uses the metaphor of the quest in arguing that learners are 'active explorers'.

The data suggests that some learners like the variety of subjects on offer, while some value the programme as a continuation of their interest in a subject which has always attracted them, in some cases professionally. As one student expressed it, picking up her professional subject (she was a teacher of literature) was a way of 'completing circles'. For others, it is the variety of topics that appeals. Others welcome the opportunity to take up a subject they never had the chance to study. One student said that she saw the programme as an opportunity to access education because she had little formal education. Glendenning (1990, p. 14) confirms that one of the great advantages of learning, whether formal or informal, is that it empowers people to study subjects that they did not have an opportunity to pursue during their earlier lives. That is, it seems to me, a profound, poignant and dynamic revelation about older learners' motivations.

The opportunity to engage in a process of lifelong learning

Nechvoglod and Beddie (2010) also stress the importance of learners identifying their own goals in terms of building their 'persistence' over a sustained time period. A salient feature of our Open Learning Programme is that the majority of our students are 'returners'; they come back to us year after year. That would suggest that, regardless of whether the motivation is to continue along a subject path or to try new subjects, there is a strong investment in the idea that learning is a lifelong process. Indeed, one student identified this specifically, by saying that engagement with the Open Learning Programme was a 'natural continuation of learning'. Research carried out by Panayotoff (1993) suggested that wellbeing benefits did not continue after older people had participated in a particular adult education programme. This perhaps points to the importance of 'persistence' – learners returning to a programme year after year, building up a habit of learning and, indeed, a learning voyage. The process, then, takes place over a long time and that is, I think, why it is effective as well as affective.

Having a structure for learning

Some learners expressed the view that having a regular programme to come along to created a structure for their learning and increased their motivation to learn in a more systematic and deeper way than they would have without the framework of classes. Being part of the programme made it easier to learn and study, because there was a regular routine of classes. For others, having a framework was more to do with being able to return each year to reconnect with their favourite subject, or to try a completely new subject in a structured way. A study carried out by Park et al. (2014) demonstrated that those who were engaged in challenging learning activities showed improvements in memory compared to those engaged in non-demanding activities at home.

The appropriateness of the teaching and learning styles

Standards of teaching

Some students said that they had enrolled because of the reputation of the programme. Many learners praised the standard of teaching, identifying especially the breadth and depth of knowledge that tutors brought to their subject, but also their willingness to engage with students. One student commented that 'a strong feature of all lecturers – I have noticed is that they are very accomplished, knowledgeable, approachable and friendly'. Students then also choose which courses to do based on the regard in which they hold particular tutors. Some students thus 'follow' tutors whose teaching and learning approach they find especially appealing and appropriate.

Participation or transmission?

In relation to the teaching and learning styles, most respondents registered approval of 'participative, seminar-style' learning. One person liked the balance between getting information and informal learning where the knowledge of the learners themselves could be drawn upon. As one student put it, 'it varies a lot – in smaller classes it is more open-ended, not so didactic. We get information and can be creative, interactive. I like the informality.' In pedagogic theory we might characterise this as a balance between 'constructivist' or 'participative', active learning approaches and 'transmissive' or 'instructionist' approaches (Jonassen, 1991). Put simply, teachers can act as the authoritative experts, transmitting knowledge to students, or work with learners to construct the learning, drawing upon the knowledge and experience they already have.

Variety of teaching styles

In terms of the variety of learning styles, some students liked the range of styles they were exposed to across different courses and also within 'panel'-taught courses, like World Literature and the Blackbird Bookclub. In relation to the first, I think this goes back to the idea that students appreciated being able to choose their own learning pathway or journey, studying a variety of topics and subjects over many years, and thus experiencing a variety not only of subjects but also of pedagogic approaches. In relation to the second, we might say that panel-taught courses, involving a variety of teaching and learning styles, deliver, in microcosm, the same notion of picking and choosing between styles or approaches but within the same subject. Of course, there is also the implicit imperative among older learners – not especially highlighted in the responses – that they are very open to a range of teaching styles, but they appreciate also a sort of anchorage too, where the convenor of panel courses acts both on their behalf and on behalf of the guest tutors. I mean by this that the class is encouraged to suggest both topics and particular tutors whom they know to be tried and tested. At the same time, the class invests in the convenor the responsibility to also challenge what is familiar, what they know and who they know, by introducing new topics and new tutors. In practice, this works out as a blend of reassuring topics or texts with which they are familiar and tutors who they know and like with a bit of risk taking, topics or texts they have not covered before (in all the years) and tutors who are a bit of an unknown quantity. To reel back a little bit, when we consider the issue of teaching and learning styles we need to relate this to the imperative, expressed again and again by learners, of being able to choose their own individual learning pathways or journeys. We need to think about this not only in terms of the content or subject but also in terms of the mode or style of the teaching and learning.

Courses responding to student wishes − co-constructing the curriculum

Students also valued the fact that the course they took was responsive to their suggestions and ideas. This has to do with students being empowered to shape the curriculum. So, for example, in all the courses I teach, I ask the students to 'recommend' books they would like to discuss, while in a music course, the tutor responded to a student's suggestion about the 'theme' for the next lecture series. This would suggest that students like to be involved not only in discussing the material but also in setting the agenda for the curriculum. This kind of student engagement is recommended by educational theorists (Nechvoglod and Beddie, 2010; Rushton and Suter, 2012, p. 16; Healey, Flint and Harrington, 2014), but as Trowler and Trowler (2010) point out, this is not always delivered in reality.

Freedom from pressure: the joy of learning for its own sake

It is also true to say that the Open Learning Programme is free of the sometimes agonising imperatives of degree courses or, indeed, school curricula; students in the programme do not have to sit internal or external examinations, and there is not, in the same sense, a set of defined 'benchmarks' or 'standards' which students must work to achieve or fail, though the programme is rigorously moderated internally and externally to ensure that standards are maintained. In common with many extramural or continuing education or lifelong learning programmes, learners come because they want to, not because their parents want them to, or because they are pursuing the programmes primarily to get a job. The older academic term for this is 'liberal education'. And what that meant, I think, was that education − even if it is for a degree − should not just be about learning the narrow, technical skills and knowledge associated with a particular 'profession'. An engineer should know something of literature; an English teacher should know something about science. Now, interestingly, interdisciplinary studies – for example, medicine and humanities – are becoming rather fashionable, perhaps in recognition that there are many ways to look at the same problem or issue and that we need to be more imaginative, to do some 'blue sky thinking'. But what I am getting at is something deeper than this, and that is a sense, understood away back in the day, and indeed, even in our own time, that learning is something to be enjoyed; that we, as human beings, are in a place of learning, not just to do the minimum required amount of reading, pass exams and get our 'piece of paper', but to discover some passion, some real love of the subject. The Open Learning Programme, like other extramural programmes, as discussed by our learners, is posited upon giving full rein to that aspect of learning, often not quite fully realised in the 'normal' higher education framework.

Size of class: implications for teaching and learning styles

Learners tended to distinguish between large lecture-style classes and smaller group seminar-style modes. Most of the responses indicated that students prefer a smaller class to a large lecture setting, and this was linked to the level of participation possible in each setting. Clearly, it is easier to operate a more active learning mode with a small group in a seminar-style setting than in a large, tiered lecture theatre. But is it desirable? One respondent extolled the more interactive learning mode because it was so different from the 'authoritarian' way in which she had been taught at school. In the past 40 or 50 years the emphasis within schools and universities has shifted towards a more 'constructivist' approach; the reality, I suspect, is that in schools and indeed in the Open Learning Programme, some tutors favour a more 'instructionist' approach while others encourage more discussion, but some tutors would, in fact, use a mixed mode, where they try to achieve a balance between imparting new knowledge to the students and enabling and empowering them to comment, analyse and discuss within a more 'constructivist' philosophy.

Teaching and learning styles in large classes

Most of the classes within the Open Learning Programme are relatively small, typically 15–20 students – that is, in terms of current educational thinking about active and participative learning, an ideal situation. But there are a few classes which are larger (40–50 students) and one which is extremely large; this is 'World Literature'. So, it may be useful to say a little more about this rather 'special case'. The class was started over 40 years ago by Dr Edith Newman-Devlin, now, sadly, no longer with us. As it happens, I 'inherited' the class and some 400 people attend each year. I note this to emphasise, yet again, a salient aspect of this programme, and I suspect many others like it, and that is the phenomenon of the very charismatic tutor. In this case, Dr Devlin was legendary and attracted hundreds of students each year. And that is the key; students returned year after year. Dr Devlin not only was a gifted teacher in her own right but also introduced, through guest lecturers, a variety of teaching styles. She also went beyond the syllabus, organising study tours to all manner of exotic locations, from Russia to Italy and France. Some students had been with her for 40 years. Nobody could take her place. And any new person must both respect what has gone before, acknowledging the importance of continuity and building trust, and, inevitably, do things in a different style and voice. For our learners, continuity and building trust with a lecturer are vital, and again this is a unique aspect of extramural programmes, utterly different from the norm of mainstream programmes, where the lecturers are the same, but the student body is different each year.

A class like World Literature has to take place in a large tiered theatre. This presents the same opportunities and challenges as any very large undergraduate degree course class in that tutors wrestle with the problem of how to make the learning more active and participatory. Some very innovative solutions have been proposed and piloted, including greater use of multimedia materials, or breaking the class into small groups to work on mini-tasks or problems (Surrency Dallas and Marwitz, 2003). Would these approaches work with World Literature? It is clear from evaluations that the learners do like visual material, such as PowerPoint presentations or playing film clips; they also like tutors who set them tasks and ask them questions.

It is also true to say that this group of students like talks which do not necessarily involve a huge amount of the sort of interactive discussion which is common in smaller classes, but in which the tutor makes reference to experiences, events or memories with which the learners can identify. This could be either curricular – for example, choosing to do a poem or novel which they studied at school – or/and it could be contrasting responses to a text which they had read at 20 to how they feel about that same text now. Some tutors are older and so can share common recollections or engage with the learners around how certain values or mores have changed across 40 or 50 years. But other tutors are appreciated because they simply communicate great passion and knowledge, and if they are witty or eloquent, so much the better. And, indeed, this ability to 'perform', to go further than simply transmitting new knowledge, but to treat the learners to the exploration of a writer in a style that is itself an example of beautiful and entertaining prose, that is crucially important. I think that older learners, especially, value more than one approach; they like the old-fashioned passionate and articulate approach because that 'fires' them to enjoy and also to think more deeply, in more complex ways, about what they are studying. White and Gardner (2012) offer some very interesting insight into what makes for the 'classroom x-factor'.

McIntyre (2003) also foregrounds the importance of the lecturing style, suggesting that students can actually enjoy large lecture theatre lectures when the lecturer(s) are prepared to deviate a little from the ground rules, including using two lecturers and getting the students to act out certain characters or concepts. In World Literature such dramatic devices have been used as well as occasional linguistic deviation by myself, perhaps using dialect now and again with a sort of knowing wink to the learners.

Teaching and learning styles in smaller classes

Interactive, 'constructivist', active learning approaches are more obviously feasible in smaller classes. The opportunity to think for oneself was cited as a particular virtue of the more interactive mode. One student found it 'informative and creative. It is always enlightening, fresh and conscientiously prepared'.

For some learners, the advantage of smaller groups and a more participative learning style was that this fostered a more critical perspective on the material, encouraging analysis. Thus, in such an approach, the goal was, according to one learner, to teach people 'to make sense of the information they already have, to analyse it'. Another student was very enthusiastic about the seminar-style format because it allowed for debate, for airing different points of view: 'I love it and that's an understatement, because in the past I have left loads of things because they have been so restrictive about the learning style. There is freedom of expression with the groups.' A study of learners in the Young at Heart College in Singapore (Lee, Wei and Hu, 2014) suggests that older people learning together develop greater self-confidence and also autonomy as learners, perhaps because they can choose what they want to learn, which brings us back to our earlier finding about learners valuing the opportunity to self-direct their learning.

Valuing the learners' previous knowledge, skills and experience

Within this, some students appreciated the fact that tutors valued the previous knowledge and experience of the learner: 'the lecturers always prepare an analysis and a point of view and then we can go on from there . . . it is skilfully led, we are allowed to speak and interact.' This comment suggests that students like an approach which, in effect, blends transmissive and constructivist elements – new knowledge is imparted, but learners are enabled to discuss and even disagree among themselves or with the tutor. The tutor or convenor attunes to the 'body of the Kirk' by listening, by engaging with the learners, and equally, 'the body of the Kirk' accepts the notion of challenge from the tutor or convenor in terms of topics or in terms of a teaching/learning approach. It is a negotiation, often implicit, sometimes explicit. In a world where older people are often dismissed, devalued or denigrated, the sense of being listened to, the sense of having their voices heard and the sense of their being tested, challenged, just as they are challenging us, are critical. As Denton (1993, p. 198) argues, 'self-directed learners have a reservoir of life experiences to bring to the learning environment.' This is at the heart of what we referred to earlier as andragogy. Learning from other students as well as from the teacher emerges as an important feature. Indeed, my own experience is that I am constantly learning from the learners, drawing upon their wide and varied experience. This kind of co-learning or collaborative pedagogy is related to co-construction of the curriculum, a way of fore-grounding and valuing learners' knowledge and experience and is a central aspect of participative andragogy (Buber, 1947; Sheridan, 1989; Imel, 1991).

One student said that participating made her more aware of her own talents. This was an especially touching response and does demonstrate how engagement with education and learning can release the potential of individuals, contribute to their 'self-actualisation' and raise their self-esteem. To learn that you do have talents is a truly empowering outcome.

Teaching and learning styles for older learners?

Should there be particular teaching and learning styles for older learners? There is a fair amount of literature, books and articles written by academic experts, suggesting that, yes, there should. Indeed, there is a specific term for teaching and learning in relation to older learners, 'gerontagogy'. The word was invented away back in 1962 by an academic called Otto Bollnow, but is only really becoming popular in the past few years (Lemieux and Martinez, 2000; Schmidt-Hertha, Krašovec and Formosa, 2014). Our data on this question did include one subtle comment which was 'age-related'; one student noted with approbation that the teaching style was 'appropriate to the age group'. But what does this mean? Findsen (2005, p. 141) argues for the importance of a humanistic approach in learning, formal or informal, and that any form of learning, informal or formal, should emphasise freedom, autonomy and individual growth. Withnal and Percy (1994) argue that pedagogical approaches should make use of the life experience of older adults. Ways should be sought to identify, acknowledge, value, use, share and build on this experience for the benefit of both individuals and groups of older learners. And there is no doubt that an interactive, facilitative teaching and learning style is most likely to create opportunities for learners to draw upon and share their life experience with the 'teacher' and with their fellow learners. Featherstone and Hepworth (2005, p. 360) point to the importance of learning styles that are more 'post-modern and diverse', as a challenge against consumer culture. I take it to be that this means fostering a learning and teaching style which encourages students to be active and critical learners, not just passive consumers of learning. Interestingly, they link this with an imperative towards promoting and constructing positive images of older people – as questioning and able to counteract negative stereotypes.

Gray (1980, p. 31) also criticises a teacher-centred ethos, because it is based on the assumption that learning is a one-way process and the expectation that students will be passive recipients. He welcomes the 'loss of control' as expert because it enables the teacher to become a facilitator of learning and to engage students more fully. Such an interactive approach, he argues, develops students' critical powers, discrimination and analysis of their own experiences.

Very interestingly, Gray (1980, p. 32) also draws attention to what we might call the emotional side of learning. He prizes 'affective' teaching which can modify attitudes, dispositions and feelings, raising the wellbeing and spirits of the learner. As he points out, such virtues are not valued by a cognitive or instructional model. His contention that learning is infectious is well supported by our data (Gray, 1980, p. 38). But 'affective teaching' does not imply that the teacher just lolls around and lets a completely unstructured discussion take place. For Gray (1980, p. 41), the teacher is a director of studies, making suggestions for lines of enquiry where resources can be found. So, there are certain instructional elements here too. The importance of giving praise is also emphasised. Nor does he shy away from suggesting that good teaching is also about a love of people (Gray, 1980, p. 33, 42). I heartily agree, and as he says, teachers need to connect at a real human level with their students, not scare them. And he also argues, rightly, that learning must be both relevant to the learner and enjoyable (Gray, 1980, p. 42).

Rushton and Suter (2012, p. 5) offer another, related, piece of advice about good practice when they advise that the teacher needs to bring herself or himself 'back to the zone of the learner'. Older people, they argue, can be our guide, and they sensibly note that disasters are inevitable; that is how we learn. And we should keep on asking the learners, encourage them to ponder, meditate, think – in other words to be 'reflective' learners, examining how and what and why they learn. This approach would echo Featherstone and Hepworth's critique of a 'managerialised discourse', where learners are simply customers and teachers are technicians (Rushton and Suter (2012, pp. 88–89).

Hiemstra (1992, p. 40) argues that the teacher should be aware that older people learn in different ways and they should allow for adequate response time, using recognition rather than recall techniques, provide adequate feedback on learner progress and employ self or peer evaluation techniques. Hiemstra (1992) also notes the success of initiatives like the Elderhostel movement, a confederation of provider institutions, mainly colleges and universities, that sponsor programs for people over 60, as well as websites like SeniorNet, based in San Francisco. We may also note the Osher Learning Institutes in America and U3A in Europe and elsewhere. We will return to discuss the potential of such initiatives a little later, in the conclusions and recommendations chapter (Chapter 6), but suffice it to note here that our own students did praise teaching and learning styles which went beyond the actual classroom, which enabled them to do educational fieldwork in other locations and other countries.

Nechvoglod and Beddie (2010, pp. 3–4), speaking about hard-to-reach learners, offer recommendations that are also very relevant for older learners. They argue that flexibility in design, content and delivery can increase self-directed learning, which in turn cultivates learner 'persistence'.

Pitching the learning in continuing education

The Open Learning Programme, in common with most formal and informal adult education programmes, is 'open entry'; there are no prerequisites in terms of education or qualifications. One of the consequences is that any class can contain a big range of students – some with a lot of previous knowledge or skills and others coming to the subject for the first time. How does the tutor 'pitch' the learning and how do learners interact with one another in that situation? Interestingly, the issue of 'pitch' was addressed by only one student, who commended tutors for being able to 'keep mixed levels happy'. We might rest on our laurels here, thinking that if pitch was a problem, it would have emerged in the data. Course evaluations, especially in very large courses like 'World Literature', do sometimes suggest that not every tutor always gets this right, especially guest lecturers who are meeting the students for the first time. We do brief and induct new tutors, and if problems are reported in this area, we act to mentor or guide the tutor. It must be said that it is impossible to please everybody all the time. Nonetheless, continual review and critical reflection through evaluations and informal comments from students, as well as internal and external moderation, are vital in enabling corrective action where it is needed.

The opportunity to study the subject at an appropriate level

Another way in which the question of pitch can be addressed is through having courses which explicitly acknowledge that people are at different 'levels'. One student valued the 'different levels of participation'. This would be especially true of the language classes; the learner progresses from basic knowledge to intermediate to advanced. But, of course, some learners will already have a bit of knowledge. In recognising this, students can enter at whatever level they feel comfortable with, from beginner to advanced levels.

Supplements to the class: notes and handouts and online materials

There were a few other aspects of the teaching and learning style which were commented upon by students; one was how much they liked getting supplementary materials like handouts or notes. One student said, 'This is a lovely and excellent service to us', while another noted that getting the notes allowed for further learning and reflection. In some courses, the students are given printed handouts, while in others, tutors send notes by email and also have hard copies. In mainstream undergraduate and postgraduate courses, course materials are now almost overwhelmingly accessed by students online; this would be over-restrictive for older learners, either because they do not 'do' computers, because they like a longer period to absorb the material, because they might have hearing loss or because they might not be able to attend all the classes.

Flexibility of timetabling

Other respondents noted that an attractive aspect of the programme was the flexible timetabling. By this one student meant that many courses were available both in the daytime and at night, while for another, the different lengths of semester (the autumn and winter are characteristically ten-week terms and the spring programme is a five-week term) were appealing. This short spring term was especially commended as many of the learners pursue other activities in the summer, go on holidays or look after grandchildren. There are also short courses held often at weekends. The experts also emphasise the importance of choice and flexibility for learners (Withnal and Percy, 1994). Though not specifically highlighted in the responses, anecdotal evidence from older learners would suggest that some do not like night courses, perhaps because of safety concerns or the difficulties of winter night-time travel.

Freedom from examinations

Other respondents noted that the lack of examinations was an attractive feature of their learning. This is pretty understandable in a culture where people are tested from a very early age and those in many kinds of work continue to be tested through a proliferating accountability culture. It may be added that the perception of education by many people is predicated upon their school experience, which was, for most, examinations-driven, and where, contingently, people were judged as either successes or failures. That this has contributed to creating what have been termed 'the missing millions, now alienated from engaging in lifelong learning', there can be no doubt (Glendenning, 1990, p. 19). Most obviously, people who did not 'succeed' in such systems then (and now) may have a certain reluctance to engage with anything labelled learning or education, the identity formation, coming, as it does, at such a young age, as 'failure' is extremely hard to overcome. I will return to this later in considering the issue of barriers to engagement in lifelong learning. In relation to continuous assessment, it is important for some and it is available in the majority of courses. One piece of research (Logan, 2013) interestingly suggests that testing is good for older learners.

The joy of learning as enhancing wellbeing: learning new ideas, skills and knowledge

A high proportion of the learners spoke about the sheer joy of learning. One student eloquently expressed this when he said, 'My happiest days were when I was a student, when I was learning new things . . . I have gone back to being as student, but without the exams.'

Some respondents testified that what they enjoyed most about the Open Learning Programme was the chance to find out about new ideas. Now, it must be said that this response reflects the fact that many but not all of the respondents were engaged in ideas-oriented subjects, like history and literature and music appreciation, what Hiemstra (1976, p. 228) calls 'expressive' subjects, but, it must also be said, without any sense of promoting its merits, that the Open Learning Programme as a whole offers a mix of practical or applied courses and what might be called intellectual courses. While the findings, then, might be biased somewhat towards the more traditional liberal arts end of the spectrum, it is clear that some students who were interviewed also took more practical courses. This suggests that learners are not just interested in having their own views of the world ratified and confirmed, but welcome opportunities to learn about a changing world, to keep up with it.

Many experts see this as a key element in older people's learning (Withnal and Percy, 1994; Jarvis, 2012; Rushton and Suter, 2012). As Jarvis (2012, p. 2) argues, we have to find new explanations, new knowledge, new ways of doing things – in other words, we must learn. This combines the ideas of continuing education for older adults being useful both as a coping mechanism and as life-enhancing and self-actualising. The enthusiasm of students for learning came across frequently and says as much about the fantastic attitude of the learners as about the courses. Here is how one student responded to the question, 'what have you learned?':

> Ach, Tess, now how could you quantify that? It has opened up a whole new world . . . the poetry class – it is like opening a bottle of Cordorniu. When you grow older you can lose the magnificent knowledge, but through Open Learning I have kept it up.

New knowledge or new skills?

The overwhelming majority of responses focused on specific subject knowledge. Other students answered that they had learned new skills, which included, for example, understanding of the Bible. I would conclude that some students, therefore, see knowledge and skills as the same thing. However, other students distinguished between knowledge and skills – for example, seeing practically based courses like digital photography as imparting skills while courses on subjects like history, literature or philosophy were characterised as imparting knowledge.

Broadening horizons and learning about different points of view

One student testified that he had gained insights into life, while others stated that participating in courses helped them to 'shape ideas' or to deepen their 'critical thinking process'. Another put it like this: 'I've learned through listening to the excellent lecturers, how to make my own critique of knowledge . . . in a way I was not able to do before.' Other students felt that they had learned to appreciate divergent opinions, different points of view. One respondent linked the development of critical thinking with learning to listen to and cherishing different points of view, and further linked these features with active learning and, indeed, the knowledge gained from studying the particular subject of literature: 'I like a good argument and for people to be able to express totally divergent opinions within the class and in different writing styles and subjects. It's good to be provoked.' I am reminded of that old Schweppes advertisement where the urbane leopard reminds us that he likes something with 'just a little more bite'. Another testified that she was also reading more books than ever before and that her reading is more focused.

Being able to learn as an older learner: challenging stereotypes

Looking firstly at what students said about the advantages of the programme in terms of the wellbeing of older people, many said that it was about keeping the mind active. One learner expressed this in a particularly vivacious way: reading and studying keep the brain active; they are 'gymnastics for the brain'. The responses implicitly reveal the very understandable worry that older learners have about 'losing it' – about descending into dementia. For one student, participating in the programme might not avert that situation: 'Going to a course is not going to stop you going doolally. But it does enable you to stay in touch, to explore ideas.'

It is clear that our older learners believe that engaging in the programme keeps the brain active, but it must be said that there is still some stereotypical thinking about the underlying question, can older people actually learn? The traditional view was that older people's brain function was not as good as that of young people, and there are those, including some older people, who believe this. Nearly 60 years ago, Welford (1958, p. 256) argued that physical performance in skilled tasks may demonstrate slower speed but accuracy often increases. And he adds that experience and coping strategies often minimise any age-related deficits. Similarly, he recommends that where large quantities of data are involved, older people benefit from either notes or other aids to processing the data, without overloading short-term memory. Welford concludes that there are such enormous individual differences that quite often he could find a substantial number of older people performing at a level at least equal to the average of a group of younger people. Motivation and interest have a significant effect on the learning of and performing of a skill, and even allowing for some natural 'slowing up', either physically or mentally, most tasks are well within the capacity of young and old alike. Interestingly, Welford recommends that clarity of presentation and provision of notes or reference material are helpful.

McClusky (1971a, p. 416), one of the great pioneers of older people's learning, stoutly defied the belief that older people could not learn as early as the 1970s:

> One can teach an old dog new tricks! He [sic] may not want to learn new tricks or he may think that his old tricks are good enough, but 'an old dog' can no longer hide behind an assumed lack of ability to learn as an excuse for not learning. In fact, because of his age there are probably some tricks that an old dog can learn better than a younger.

McClusky (1971b) argued that research has now demonstrated that mental growth is possible and takes place during the later years. He identified the need for transcendence – rising above age-related limitations, as well as a 'community of generations' (McClusky, 1978, p. 50). Perhaps in that, too, he was a sage, seeing into the future: that a generation 'gap' was opening which would one day pit the young and old against one another, as some present-day commentators and politicians seem determined to do. Jarvis (1995, p. 6), 20 years later, reprises McClusky's canine metaphor. He cites Sherron and Lumsden (1978), Allman (1982) and Glendenning and Percy (1990), who all argue that the elderly can and do learn effectively, even if their methods of learning may be slightly different.

And contemporary science is encouraging. Tyler (2011), for example, argues that the traditional view (that normal ageing involves changes in the brain which lead to problems with memory, attention and problem solving) needs to change. A more positive view is emerging in which ageing is no longer seen as an inexorable progressive decline in neural and cognitive fitness. She demonstrates that there is enormous variability in the decline of mental abilities. The research argues that brain health is what matters most, and that this can be maintained as age increases. She suggests that the traditional view of the causal link between age and cognitive decline is incorrect. The link is between brain health and cognitive decline. Especially relevant to what we have tentatively suggested about older people 'internalising' negative images of what being old is like, Tyler found that older people who conform to negative stereotyping of ageing were more likely to suffer negative impact on their cognitive functioning. So, perhaps, what the learners are really saying (or one of the things they are saying) is that conceding or 'giving in' to the idea that they are old will make them behave as if they are mentally in decline, incapable of learning.

Withnal and Percy (1994) also assert the importance of challenging negative stereotypes presenting older people as passive, non-productive, intellectually declining or non-educable, stating that older people internalise these stereotypes. Withnal (2004, p. 93) challenges the whole set of myths about older people learning and musters evidence-based arguments to debunk the myths – for example, 'older people are all the same'; 'older people have less brain capacity'; 'older people are too slow to learn anything new.'

Writing from a more academic educational point of view, Staehelin (2005, p. 175) also argues that the most important factors in the prevention of cognitive decline are education and continuing use of intellectual faculties. Promoting health and wellbeing in old age depends crucially on the educational opportunities in a population. This view is endorsed by Wolf (2009, p. 60). She quotes many sources to back up her assertion that 'there is increasing evidence that older adults who are stimulated mentally experience less decline in memory, and continued growth in verbal knowledge well into their late seventies'. And another expert in lifelong learning and continuing education, Field (2012), argues for benefits to cognitive function that can arise from learning. There is much here to encourage older people to reject the now obsolete idea that they are incapable of learning.

Enhancing wellbeing and keeping the brain active through specific subjects

In relation to the benefits of studying particular subjects, there is some interesting research. Some experts argue that learning a new language is especially beneficial for older learners. For example, a study by Bak *et al.* (2014) provided data about 853 participants who were tested at age 11 and again at ages 73–75. It showed a positive impact of learning a second language on cognition, including the onset of dementia. Others extol the virtues of music, especially in terms of older people playing music ('Learning', 2011; J. Groake, 2015).

The special courses; wellbeing for some

Level of uptake and reactions to 'ageing' stereotypes

The uptake of the special courses on ageing was not huge: 'Representations of Older People: Tattered Coat or Business Coat' attracted 14 students; 'Creative Writing: Voyages around Memory' had 27 students; 'School Days: The

Best Years of Your Life' had 9 students; 'Pass Me the Jam: Ageing Positively' had 6 students. These are small numbers within an overall student enrolment for the spring 2014 programme of 1,555.

Among those who did not enrol, the reasons given were various; some said they didn't see them listed in the brochure, and this may be because, while there was information at the front of the brochure alerting students to the special courses, the course descriptions appeared in different subject sections. Those learners who tend to concentrate on one subject area may not, therefore, have spotted them. Leaflets about the special courses were also distributed among a range of classes before the end of the winter term, but, again, it is clear that not all students were aware of them. In retrospect, the courses might have been more effectively promoted. A number of learners felt that they already knew how to 'do' older age, but others expressed the view that they did not feel that they were ageing. I suspect that part of the rejection of courses to do with ageing was also to do with the frequently negative stereotypes of older people which are projected in the media and, indeed, in political discourse. The characterisation of older people as a burden, decrepit or incapable is one which older learners very understandably wish to repudiate. This, coupled with the comments about successful negotiation of retirement and thus the lack of need for courses on ageing, reveals a kind of resistance among older learners to an explicit focus on ageing. However, one student did say that she would be interested in later-life ageing.

Another student said that she associated the Open Learning Programme with rejuvenation. And this intriguing remark was echoed in responses to other questions when students spoke about the virtues of the programme as enhancing their wellbeing by keeping the brain active and acting as a kind of brake on the mental and physical deterioration popularly associated with ageing. Thus, while learners resisted too much focus on ageing, they saw the programme nonetheless as addressing some of the potential difficulties of ageing.

Of those who did participate, they offered as reasons the hope of getting more information and to see what was on offer for older people and the opportunity to share ideas and experience of retirement with others. Interestingly, one of the learners said that she had enrolled because she did not feel comfortable with the current representations of older people: 'nowadays, the media present the ageing population as causing us difficulties.' While some students avoided the courses because of a rejection of cultural stereotypes, one took a special course for the same reason. One student said that she chose two of the courses because she liked the style of teaching offered by the two lecturers concerned. And this goes back to a point made earlier; some students tended to follow not only the same subjects each year but also particular lecturers whose teaching style they liked.

Experience of the special courses

But what kind of experience did students have who enrolled on the special courses? Most had positive things to say. One student thought that the course on the representation of older people in literature raised her awareness; another liked the interactive style, where students were encouraged to relate the books to their own experience.

There was one candidly negative response from a learner who had been a peer tutor in one of the other courses, 'Pass Me the Jam: Healthy Ageing'. She felt that she had been 'preaching to the converted'; this echoes the earlier comments from students who felt that they knew already how to model ageing or retirement. It would have been easy to suppress the negative or ambivalent comments, to omit 'data' which is discouraging or which suggests, at least to some extent, failure, but we are of the view that we must honestly reflect what learners say, even though it might not suit our hopes and expectations. We greatly hoped that by generating and delivering a set of special courses on ageing which were, in fact, questioning prevailing attitudes, most especially negative stereotypes of ageing, that we could offer our learners something that would resonate with them in terms of drawing out both the positives and negatives of becoming older. That the magic did not always work, even for those who attended, must be honestly acknowledged. In reflecting truthfully what learners said about the special courses, we are following academic experts like Cook (2009) and Quicke (2010), who use the term 'messy research' to denote an approach to research which suggests that researchers need to be, above all, truthful, and not bend the data to bolster a particular preconceived idea of what the researcher wants to hear from the research 'subjects'.

Interestingly, most of the tutors reported that being involved on the courses was a very positive experience. Tutors noted that participants were keen and welcoming. Two said that everyone 'had ownership' and students were willing to get involved. One saw the courses as an opportunity to challenge the negative stereotypes of older people as a burden on society, and rather to demonstrate their creativity, critical skills and resilience.

Tutors also felt that the learners had a lot to bring to the subject of ageing and that they were learning as much from each other as they were from the tutor, but were also more than capable of learning new skills. Tutors enjoyed the non-hierarchical relationship with students. In relation to the Schooldays course, the tutor commented on the positive response from students to 'the opportunity to reflect on their own experience of school, and to compare it with the experience of their children and grandchildren'. Another tutor concluded that 'we should cherish our older people and understand how they can teach us'. In a similar vein, one tutor argued that the courses 'helped unpack the monolithic notion of old age' and reveal the 'precious resource that older people represent, and how they can teach us'. In terms of whether the courses enhanced older people's wellbeing, one tutor commented, in relation to the memoir course, that as people get older they become more interested in 'knowing' and having a properly organised account of where they came from to pass on to the next generations. Others commented on the importance of the participants 'learning that they have a voice'.

Conclusions about specific courses on ageing

We may conclude that older learners are not attracted in large numbers to courses focusing on ageing, though they do believe that the Open Learning Programme, as a whole, does have a positive effect on the wellbeing of older learners. So, perhaps the reality is that older learners feel bombarded by negative stereotyping about ageing and that these cultural constructions have become internalised within older people, so that they want to dissociate themselves from *self-images* as burdensome, dependent and decrepit. Hiemstra's research (1976) suggests that older people are interested in learning that practically addresses effective mastery of old age challenges. While some of our learners hinted that others might benefit from this kind of learning, they did not identify it as relevant to themselves and were rather more interested in what Hiemstra (1976, p. 228) terms 'expressive learning' – literature, arts and crafts, subjects which enhance enjoyment of life.

One student noted that a focus on ageing 'becomes therapeutic, making ageing seem a very serious matter – it reminds me of the approach of the Grim Reaper and one prefers to avoid that realisation'. One student expressed the view of several that such courses could actually constitute a barrier and that the courses were already catering for older people. Another learner, however, did comment on the research project more generally, wishing us luck with it and praising the project because it gave learners an end goal and a product. And one student did say that she would be interested in a course 'relating to coping skills when you get older, how to avoid dementia', though she 'would not be rushing to courses which focused on diet and nutrition', but currently, she is more interested in 'knowledge-based courses'. Perhaps one of the most astute comments was that 'the programme itself is already addressing this aspect'. And this was echoed by another student who said that 'there are enough elements in existing courses to cover this'. One student noted that courses should 'discuss the positives of retirement – the freedom to do what you want to do and the freedom to travel'. A similar sentiment was expressed by another learner who said that she would like special courses only 'if ageing was presented in a positive light – how to get the most out of life'.

Within the academic community, there have been many articles and books written about 'positive' ageing. But I suspect that our learners are like most students in informal and indeed formal education programmes and do not come across this academic literature, because they are pursuing subjects which interest them and from which they derive enjoyment. Yet, when a set of special courses is offered, drawing implicitly on this academic literature, but mostly 'embedding' it pretty deeply, or if you will, disguising the theory beneath the subject – literature or history – the response of our students is still by no means overwhelmingly positive. The more regrettable – and ironic – aspect of this, evidenced by the data, is that older learners do not realise how much the academics in areas like educational gerontology are so powerfully on their side in passionately arguing for the value of learning in positive ageing. We will have a little more to say about that shortly. Here, I want to draw attention to how, in the absence of knowing about all these terrific allies and what they have said, older learners are, the data would suggest, very much influenced by negative popular media and political representations of ageing. Only one learner urged us to 'keep going with the special courses'.

Conclusion

It seems, then, that for our learners, special courses on ageing are not the way forward. And we must respect the views of the learners. How to close the gap, the synapses, between the affirming perspectives coming from educational gerontology and cultural gerontology and the understandable ambivalence of older learners to focus on ageing is a question which yields no easy answer. Perhaps this book may help older learners to realise that they are not alone and that they have the best of friends as well as more ignominious detractors.

Certain it is that older learners are wise and crystalline about what they do want from an education programme, and what they would wish to change. They welcome being able to direct their own learning, to choose their learning pathway. This highlights the point made earlier about the uniqueness and individuality of older people. They are not all the same, not just a homogenous 'other'. They appreciate being involved in a process of lifelong learning; they like having a structure or framework for learning, a regular and sustained contact with education. Our students enjoy a variety of teaching styles but appreciate especially the opportunity to actively contribute and, indeed, to help shape and co-construct the curriculum. The learners expressed their sense of validation from having their varied experience and knowledge valued – as young people would say, 'respected'. Some learners pointed to aspects of the learning experience which they felt to be appropriate to older learners. Lecture and seminar notes and backup materials delivered in both hard copy and by email were appreciated. Freedom from exams, flexible timetabling, pitching classes to take account of a range of expertises, being able to study a subject at different levels, new knowledge, new skills, broadening horizons and being able to learn as older learners were all cited as positive features of the programme. And for some students, the chance to pursue particular subjects may specifically add to wellbeing. But above all, what emerged was the sheer joy of learning, as is evident in Figures 3.1 and 3.2. And, surely, that is a precious process.

Figure 3.1 Open Learning Programme student Jay Holmes considers images of ageing, quizzical.

Figure 3.2 Open Learning Programme student Bill Love ponders Yeats: of what is past, passing and to come.

References

Bak, T.H., Nissan, J.J., Allerhand, M.M. and Deary, I.J. (2014) 'Does bilingualism influence cognitive aging?', *Annals of Neurology*, 75 (6), pp. 959–963.

Buber, M. (1947) *Between man and man*, Smith, R.G. trans., London: Kegan Paul.

Cook, T. (2009) 'The purpose of mess in action research: Building rigour through a messy turn', *Educational Action Research*, 17 (2), pp. 277–291.

Denton, V.L. (1993) *Booker T. Washington and the adult education movement*, Gainesville, FL: University Press of Florida.

Featherstone, M. and Hepworth, M. (2005) 'Images of ageing: Cultural representations of later life', in Johnson, M.L. (ed.) *The Cambridge handbook on age and ageing*, Cambridge: Cambridge University Press, pp. 354–362.

Field, J. (2012) 'Lifelong learning, welfare and mental well-being into older age: Trends and policies in Europe', in Boulton-Lewis, G. and Tam, M. (eds.) *Active ageing, active learning: Issues and challenges* (Education in the Asia-Pacific Region: Issues, Concerns and Prospects), New York: Springer, pp. 11–19.

Findsen, B. (2005) *Learning later*, Malabar, FL: Kreiger Publishing Company.

Glendenning, F. (1990) 'The emergence of educational gerontology', in Glendenning, F. and Percy, K. (eds.) *Ageing, education and society: Readings in educational gerontology*, Keele, Staffordshire: Association for Educational Gerontology, pp. 13–23.

Glendenning, F. (1995) *Learning and cognition in later life: Studies in educational gerontology 2*, Farnham, Surrey: Ashgate Publishing.

Gray, R.J. (1980) 'How do you teach the elders?', in Glendenning, F. (ed.) *Outreach education and the elders: Theory and practice*, Stoke on Trent: Beth Johnson Foundation Publications and Department of Adult Education, University of Keele, pp. 31–44.

Groake, J. (2015) 'Participants required for study on the effects of music on the ageing brain' [online]. Available at http://www.nuigalway.ie/about-us/news-and-events/news-archive/2015/november2015/participants-required-for-study-of-the-effects-of-music-on-the-ageing-brain.html (Accessed: 7 December 2015).

Healey, M., Flint, A. and Harrington, K. (2014) *Engagement through partnership: Students as partners in learning and teaching in higher education*, York: Higher Education Academy.

Hiemstra, R. (1976) 'Older learning: Instrumental and expressive categories', *Educational Gerontology*, 1, pp. 227–236.

Hiemstra, R. (1992) 'Aging and learning: An agenda for the future', in Tuijnman, A.C. and Van der Kamp, M. (eds.) *Learning across the lifespan: Theories, research, policies*, Oxon: Pergamon Press, pp. 53–70.

Imel, S. (1991) 'Collaborative learning in adult education', *ERIC Digest*, 113, unpaged.

Jarvis, P. (1995) *Adult and continuing education: Theory and practice*, 2nd edn, Oxon: Routledge.

Jarvis, P. (2012) 'Learning from everyday life', *HSSRP*, 1 (1), pp. 1–20 [online]. Available at http://hssrp.uaic.ro/continut/1.pdf (Accessed: 7 December 2015).

Jonassen, D.H. (1991) 'Objectivism vs. constructivism', *Educational Technology Research and Development*, 39 (3), pp. 5–14.

Knowles, M.S. and associates. (1984) *Andragogy in action: Applying modern principles of adult learning*, San Francisco, CA: Josey-Bass.

'Learning an instrument "helps older people"'. (2011) *British Psychological Society Research Digest* [online]. Available at http://www.bps.org.uk/news/learning-instrument-helps-older-people (Accessed: 2 July 2014).

Lee, Y., Wei, H. and Hu, M. (2014) 'An exploration in the learning processes of retirees in Singapore', *Contemporary Educational Research Quarterly*, 22 (3), pp. 91–30.

Lemieux, A. and Martinez, M.S. (2000) 'Gerontagogy beyond words: A reality', *Educational Gerontology*, 26, pp. 475–498.

Logan, J. (2013) 'Testing helps both young and old to learn', *British Psychological Society News* [online]. Available at http://www.bps.org.uk/news/testing-helps-both-young-and-old-learn (Accessed: 4 August 2014).

McClusky, H.Y. (1971a) 'The adult as learner', in Seashore, S.E. and McNeill, R.J. (eds.) *Management of the urban crises*, New York: The Free Press, pp. 27–39.

McClusky, H.Y. (1971b) *Education: Background paper for 1971 White House conference on aging*, Washington, DC: White House Conference on Ageing. Available at http://files.eric.ed.gov/fulltext/ED057335.pdf (Accessed: 27 December 2015).

McClusky, H.Y. (1978) 'The community of generations: A goal and a context for the education of persons in the later years', in Sherron, R.H. and Lumsden, D.B. (eds.) *Introduction to educational gerontology*, Washington, DC: Hemisphere Publishing Corporation, pp. 59–84.

McIntyre, D. (2003) 'Using foregrounding theory as a teaching methodology in a stylistics course', *Pedagogy of Style and Stylistics*, 37 (1), pp. 1–13.

Nechvoglod, N. and Beddie, F. (2010) 'Equality in VET: Good practice principles' [online]. Available at https://scholar.google.co.uk/scholar?cluster=111547670383 69655091&hl=en&as_sdt=0,5 (Accessed: 4 August 2014).

Panayotoff, K.G. (1993) 'The impact of continuing education on the health of older adults', *Journal of Educational Gerontology*, 19 (1), pp. 9–20.

Park, D., Lodi-Smith, J., Drew, L., Haber, S., Hebrank, A., Bischof, G.N. and Aamodt, W. (2014) 'The impact of sustained engagement on cognitive function in older adults: The synapse project,' *Psychological Science*, 25 (1), pp. 103–112.

Quicke, J. (2010) 'Narrative strategies in educational research: Reflections on critical autoethnography', *Educational Action Research*, 18 (2), pp. 239–254.

Rushton, I. and Suter, M. (2012) *Reflective practice for teaching in lifelong learning*, Berks.: Open University Press.

Schmidt-Hertha, B., Jelenc Krašovec, S. and Formosa, M. (eds.) (2014) *Learning across generations in Europe: Contemporary issues in older adult education*, Rotterdam, Boston and Taipei: Sense Publishers.

Sheridan, J. (1989) 'Rethinking andragogy: The case for collaborative learning in continuing higher education', *The Journal of Continuing Higher Education*, 37 (2), pp. 2–6.

Staehelin, H.B. (2005) 'Promoting health and wellbeing in later life', in Johnson, M.L. (ed.) *The Cambridge handbook on age and ageing*, Cambridge: Cambridge University Press, pp. 165–180.

Surrency Dallas, P. and Marwitz, M.R. (2003) 'Community or contact zone? Deconstructing an honors classroom', *Pedagogy*, 3 (3), pp. 435–439.

Trowler, P. and Trowler, V. (2010) *Student engagement evidence summary*, York: Higher Education Academy.

Tyler, L.K. (2011) 'The resilient brain: Cognition and ageing' (Joint British Academy/British Psychological Society Lecture, The Royal Society, London, 22nd September) [online]. Available at http://www.britac.ac.uk/events/2011/The_Resilient_Brain.cfm (Accessed: 2 September 2014).

Welford, A.T. (1958) *Ageing and human skills*, London: Oxford University Press.

White, J. and Gardner, J. (2012) *The classroom x-factor*, Oxon: Routledge.

Withnal, A. (2004) 'Older learners: Challenging the myths', in Withnal, A., McGivney, V. and Soulsby, J. (eds.) *Older people learning – myths and realities*, Leicester: NIACE, pp. 85–100.

Withnal, A. and Percy, K. (1994) *Good practice in the education and training of older adults*, Aldershot, Hants.: Ashgate Publishing Ltd.

Wolf, M.A. (2009) 'Learning in older adulthood', in Jarvis, P. (ed.) *The Routledge international handbook of lifelong learning*, Oxon: Routledge, pp. 56–54.

Chapter 4

Findings

The social dimensions of older people's learning

Having discussed some aspects of the educational side of wellbeing, let us now turn to the social aspect – the opportunity to meet people in class and outside class.

Complementing educational wellbeing

In looking more closely at the interview transcripts, it becomes evident that some students are not especially interested in social networks, perhaps because they already have a virtuous circle of friends or because they are not a bit interested in making friends and are happy enough with what we might call the self-actualisation or personal fulfilment of the intellectual engagement. For others, the social interaction is valued. But for many, it is the combination of intellectual and social stimulus which is valued. This is reflected in a study of the Osher Learning communities in America, where it is the holistic nature of the learning experience, enabling learners both to have a sense of ownership over their learning and to have a supporting social dimension, which is valued (Brady, Cardale and Neidy, 2013, pp. 631–632).

Wellbeing through creating social networks: friends or friendly acquaintances?

Some of the learners responded that they had not made any friends, while some said they had. Indeed, one learner reported that he had witnessed the burgeoning of a romance in his class. One learner spoke very movingly about the friendships she had made:

> It's a good lesson in ageing; we are all approaching 80 and have experienced various traumas. It is very refreshing to meet people of your own age group and nice to branch away from your own circle. We roar with laughter about the daft things we've done, discover the best lipsticks.

Several respondents said that they had not made friends so much as 'friendly acquaintances'. Thus, a distinction was drawn by quite a few between close

friendships or 'special friendships' and the kind of pleasant acknowledgement and exchange that characterised their relationships with other learners.
One respondent said, when he sees people outside the class in other social
settings, 'I greet people and make nice contacts.' Other learners noted that
they would meet before or after the class and have coffee or lunch.

Another learner said that it was a bit daunting coming along on your own
for the first time, but congratulated her particular tutor for encouraging
contributions from new students joining the class. This goes back to the data
about friendships too and how we might improve social interaction among
students, for those who feel this to be important. As one learner expressed
it, 'continuing to learn and having company in the process'. Others testified
to the advantages of collective learning: 'working in a group of like-minded
people, having meaningful and critical discussion . . . the collective aspect
is very important to me. I find it challenging, for me it represents living in
today'; 'meeting new friends, exchanging ideas encourages one to disciplined
study, keeps the mind active'; '[the programme] continues to develop participants' skills and knowledge, engaging in groups, assists with all sorts of
things as courses are in a social learning and developmental setting.'

Much has been written about the importance of combating social isolation among older people. The UK Government invested £1 million to help
those most at risk (Department for Work and Pensions, 2015) and set up
the Ageing Well Programme, devolved to local government (Local Government Association, 2012). However, education or learning is not mentioned
specifically, though there is a welcome emphasis on older people as active
citizens co-producing better outcomes. Cattan *et al.* (2005) refer to a range
of international policy documents which focus on the issue of loneliness
among older people, including the World Health Organization (2002) and
the UK Department of Health (2001). They reviewed a number of interventions and, significantly, those with an educational dimension were judged
to be the most effective. In Northern Ireland, the Assembly's Active Ageing
Strategy (2014) recognises the importance of tackling loneliness and isolation. Websites such as the Campaign to End Loneliness (2014) and the work
of the Future Foundation (2014) also demonstrate the importance of this
issue for older people. It is interesting to note that one of the New Dynamics of Ageing projects, Music for Life, specifically states that its goal is to
explore the role of participation in community music activities in promoting
social engagement and wellbeing in older people (Hallam, 2011).

The learning environment as a factor in wellbeing

What is meant by 'support'?

When we asked students about what they thought of the support services,
they interpreted this in two distinct ways. Some students understood 'support services' to mean specific services available for people with disabilities,

while others interpreted the phrase as having to do with what we might call 'front of house' – what did they think of what some academic experts have referred to as 'the learning environment'?

The question was put in the first place because we were very aware that even if teaching and learning styles are excellent, learners' wellbeing can be adversely affected because not enough care has gone into considering the learners' needs, expectations and aspirations in a holistic way. So, our sense of the question was broad, and we would have assumed students would talk to us about a range of 'environmental' issues, such as how easy it was to get to the campus; how accessible the rooms were; whether the needs of disabled learners were identified and addressed; how easy or difficult it was to enrol; how easy or difficult it was to get something changed that was annoying them; what the attitude of support staff was. There is a lesson there about language – within the university, we use the phrase 'support services' in a much more general way than people outside do, so we should have been more thoughtful about understanding that we were, in fact, using a quite specific, internal meaning of that phrase. In one sense, the fact that a number of responses understood the phrase to be about disability support points to the error of our ways, but in another way, it is encouraging to realise that our older learners are, in this day and age, tuned in to the availability of support for learners with disabilities. It must also be said that 30 years ago there was hardly an accessible building on any university campus, to say nothing of the absence in most of a unit called Disability Services. But how aware are our learners about disability services? Among those who focused on this 'reading' of the question, most seemed happy enough, one noting rightly that the university needed to be compliant with the Disability Discrimination Act (1995), implying that disability support services should be there as a matter of course. I have to say I rather liked this comment because it suggested that at least one of our learners did not feel that students had to somehow beg for adjustments which would make their participation possible. And, it must be said, beyond the data, that some students are quite vocal, in my view rightly so, about rooms which are too cold. We need to be sensitive to the fact that some older people do feel the cold more than young people, though addressing the temperature in a particular room in a centrally controlled system is not always entirely straightforward.

One or two learners also very politely complained about the problems that fixed seating caused for students with certain medical conditions. Again, this is rarely an issue for young students, and in smaller classes, the 'environment' is a bit more flexible, but in larger lecture theatres, this can be a problem. Having been made aware of this, I need to consider how this might be addressed through connecting the students concerned with Disability Services. Another student made a very interesting comment in response to the question about support services when she said, 'Older people helped other older people with lifts or going for coffee.'

Most students expressed satisfaction about the support systems. In relation to support staff, one respondent, for example, noted that staff members were 'very warm and welcoming and helpful'. Support staff and tutors are made very aware of how important it is to treat all our learners with respect and warmth, take the time to listen to any difficulties expressed by students relating to their 'environment' and address these to the best of our ability. Withnal and Percy (1994), drawing on other experts, emphasise how crucial it is for institutions to be welcoming, accessible, aware, encouraging, supportive and responsive (McGivney, 1990; Schuller and Boostyn, 1992). They also cite Hiemstra's (1992) argument that the creation of accessible and appropriate learning environments – physical and psychological/emotional – is fundamental.

Facilities

A number of students noted that they would like to see a coffee service near all classes, or even in them, as used to be the case in World Literature. One also made the point that there does not seem to be a central place for students to get directions around the campus since the Porters' Lodge was removed. There is, I should note, a visitors' centre, but some of our learners may not be aware of it, so some work could be done to alert students more about this facility.

Access to information about courses: how would learners find out about the programme?

In relation to how learners found out about the programme, interestingly, the majority said that they had first heard of the Open Learning Programme through family or friends. This perhaps tells us something about how older learners initially engage. It may be noted that the programme would run advertisements and has a wide mailing list, but personal recommendation and the use of social networks seem to be the most common form of 'advertising'. One respondent had first heard about the programme on the radio (this would have been an interview rather than direct advertising), and another had discovered it through an online search, while two learners picked up a copy of the brochure in the local library. Four learners said that, now, they find out about the courses through the brochure, which they are automatically sent. Therefore, they can read the print version or access it online. This raises some interesting questions about what are the best ways to market such programmes. We will return to this in the final chapter.

Flexible enrolment

Responses indicate that the majority of learners interviewed enrol online, while some enrol by telephone, some in person and a fewer number by post. I may note that the proportion of learners now enrolling online has risen steadily over the past few years. However, we must also bear in mind the numbers who do not and also the fact that some learners use different methods at different times. The lesson here is that learning programmes need to remain flexible and learner-centred in terms of facilitating easy access. This is a challenge, given that most university systems now expect students to conduct the business of enrolling and much else online. As noted in relation to a previous question, not all our older learners 'do' computers and we need to continue to offer flexible systems which do not create barriers for potential learners.

Geographical access

Some students cited, for example, how easy it was to get to Queen's by train, and of course, in Northern Ireland, travel is free for people of state pension age. For certain classes, like World Literature, students travel all the way from Derry/Londonderry (some two hours by train or bus) and indeed from Drogheda and Dublin (up to two hours by train or bus). One student was appreciative of the fact that the programme offered outreach courses in some areas.

However, some learners listed a number of barriers. While train and bus services are fairly good in the greater Belfast area, it must be said that it is much more difficult to get to some courses from rural areas. On a related theme, one learner said that parking was difficult to find. And there is no doubt that it is almost impossible to get a parking space right on the main campus during term time for daytime courses. However, some improvements to this are currently being made.

Affordability

Learners overwhelmingly thought that the programme was good value for money. One student succinctly expressed the general attitude: 'without doubt, peanuts.' Another student was not sure, questioning whether the courses offered by Queen's were better value than those offered by another third-level competitor in the city. One student said that classes offered through U3A were cheaper, but they did not, in her opinion, necessarily achieve the standards of the Open Learning Programme.

How could the programme further enhance the wellbeing of learners?

Social and environmental improvements

Most of the respondents professed themselves very satisfied with the programme. Of those who did want changes, many of the responses to this question were, interestingly, around what we have referred to earlier as 'environmental' issues. Some students said that they would like to have more opportunities to interact socially, either through mid-class coffee breaks or meeting outside the class. The lack of availability of facilities for tea and coffee in every class location was raised by more than one student. In relation to the physical needs of learners, it must also be acknowledged that older learners may get a bit thirsty or hungry and many of them are not habitual water bottle carriers, as is the fashion for young people. But, perhaps primarily, the desire for the coffee represents a desire to have more time to talk and get to know other people in the class. And this may be especially important for new people coming along, particularly if they are joining long-established 'core groups' of learners within classes. In practice, some tutors do create a break in a two-hour class, and mostly the learners would decide, as a group, if they wanted a break. However, depending on the location, it may not always be possible for students to get a coffee or a cup of tea. Regrettably, providers are not always masters of their destiny here, but it is certainly an issue that could be raised with learning organisations.

Some tutors, myself included, hold little parties at Christmas and sometimes also at the end of the year. For tutors teaching language and culture classes this has been a wonderful opportunity to sample the cuisine of other countries, and tutors have been very generous in supplying lots of lovely treats. The 'party' classes are, contingently, less formal and in one group, I shape this class as a kind of open forum where students can read their own poems or a poem they like or even play a bit of music or sing a song. It is a lovely chance for everybody to relax a bit and also have a bit of fun.

Barriers for those not engaging with the programme

Some learners approached the question about barriers also from the perspective of considering what barriers there might be for people not currently enrolled on the programme, and this is, in my view, one of the most important parts of the data. It is gratifying to realise that the learners do think of other older people for whom there may well be barriers.

Finding out about the programme: access to information

Our students were of the view that the programmes should be advertised more effectively. Suggestions included arranging for brochures to be available at literary events or linked to book sites as well as leaflets being available in supermarkets. One learner thought that some people might think that they had to do assignments and that might put them off. She said that this should be made clearer in the brochure – a very good point.

Perceptions of university as 'not for the likes of us'

Some learners thought that the university setting itself might deter some people, especially those who are not familiar with the area around Queen's University, or that those who did not have third-level education might feel that Queen's was not for them and only for people doing degrees or post-graduate work – that it was too academic. The learners here are honestly reflecting a perception in the community – any community – that universities are seen as elitist and only for young people. In reality, as we have noted earlier, there are no formal qualifications required and the programme is very wide-ranging, so while there are courses which may seem academic – in subjects like history or literature or philosophy – there are many in practical subjects, like learning the guitar, first aid and computers, as well as plenty of courses in leisure subjects, like golf, ceili dancing, sewing, knitting and personal development. This kind of range is, doubtless, reflected in many lifelong learning programmes, both formal and informal.

Perception may be, indeed, the main problem; how people can internalise images of themselves as not 'fit' for education and, thus, self-exclude. There are clearly complex class and cultural factors. While the levels of participation in continuing education, formal and informal, are growing, though still low as a proportion of the overall older population (Findsen, 2005, p. 71), it must be acknowledged that there are, as we have noted earlier, 'the missing millions', leaving school at 12 or 14 and never returning to education because of some or all of these factors, as observed by Glendenning (1990, p. 19). Percy (1990, p. 43) states that female, middle-class and well-educated people are more likely to participate than male, working-class people and those with no educational qualifications. Field (2005, p. 41) paints a dispiriting picture of participation rates in Northern Ireland: 'only about 30% of adult population participate in formal and informal learning. In Scotland it is 42%.' Glendenning (1990, p. 14), in noting the importance of older people retaining their intellectual faculties and continuing to participate in community life, argues also for greater 'access to fields which had not been open to them during their working life'.

One very interesting suggestion from our data was that we run more taster courses, a proposition put forward also by some experts to attract 'hard-to-reach learners' (Nechvoglod and Beddie, 2010). The taster courses could demonstrate that the programme is both accessible and enjoyable and span a wide range of topics, from wine appreciation to sewing to philosophy to science to first aid. We have done this in the past, and with some success, and, indeed, have manned stalls and distributed leaflets in all sorts of shops and businesses, but at present do not really have the staff resources to do these kinds of promotional activities. Perhaps there are ways of involving our own students as ambassadors, and we will return to this in the final chapter.

Financial barriers, caring responsibilities, ill health

There are also practical barriers for some older people, as our own students pointed out. And there may be additional 'hidden barriers' – caring responsibilities and health problems, some of them age-related. Some of our learners said they were not sure if someone on a state pension only could afford the courses. Perhaps, considering this, one learner suggested that there should be a Friends of Open Learning set up with the aim of making a fund available for widening access. At present, there is a bursary scheme, set up, as it happens, in the name of my mother, which offers assistance to those in hardship. However, this would be known only to those who check out the programme in the first instance, and it must be taken into account that those older people who have very little disposable income would simply rule out education as an option. We will return to this in the conclusions and recommendations chapter.

Conclusion

We have seen in this chapter how, for many older people, the social dimension of their learning experience is very important. While it may be hazarded that if a similar study was carried out among young people, the importance of the social dimension would also loom large in their perceptions, indeed, perhaps even more so, older people do not stop wanting to make friends or friendly acquaintances and engage with other people by participating in groups. The social dimension for many, though not all, complements their educational wellbeing. Some learners also see participating as a way of being able to bring back benefits to the younger generations, so the intergenerational richness is also a feature.

However, no matter how good the quality of the actual education is, for older people, the learning environment is also a critical factor in wellbeing. Support facilities for students with disabilities and good 'front-of-house' staff who are welcoming and take time to answer queries and respond to any issues or complaints which arise are also fundamental to the learning experience. Getting good, clear and attractive information about courses in formats which are accessible is vital, as is ensuring that promotional materials are circulated in places where older people are likely to see or hear them. As we have said many times in this book, older people are not all the same; some 'do' computers and some do not. Providers need to bear this in mind and facilitate would-be learners to access information in a format that is natural to them. Similarly, enrolling for courses needs to be enabling rather than a bureaucratic nightmare; older people appreciate being offered choice: coming along in person, enrolling by telephone, filling out a form and posting it or enrolling online. While in our Open Learning Programme an increasing number of learners do enrol online, the other modes need to be retained so that older learners keep their independence rather than having to rely on someone to download and print the information for them.

Opportunities to interact socially over coffee or a sandwich are also valued by learners, and the chance to participate in 'extramural' activities is

Figure 4.1 Open Learning Programme student Trevor Walker. Jokes occur even for – especially for – older people.

welcomed, though it is recognised that staff are often stretched. We will return to this in the final chapter.

Our learners pinpointed a number of barriers to learning for other older people not currently engaged. These included a lack of information about the courses and a perception that university-based courses were likely to be too academic and above the reach of ordinary people. More needs to be done to actively promote learning programmes. Affordability is a barrier for millions of older people. As we saw in the introduction, many older people live in poverty and even the modest cost of a course is beyond their means. And it is not just the cost of the course itself; transport, respite or other support costs need to be factored in. For other older people, poor health or caring responsibilities constitute barriers. Learning providers cannot solve all these problems, but closer joined-up thinking at the governmental level could lead to more imaginative solutions, such as education in the community, including within residential homes and sheltered housing.

As we will see in our concluding chapter, the overall wellbeing benefits for and with older people engaging in learning are becoming increasingly evident. All of us can share these benefits by enabling older people to enhance their wellbeing and wisdom as a resource for us all. Older learners have much to teach us about the medicinal values of laughter, as can be seen in Figures 4.1 and 4.2.

Figure 4.2 Open Learning Programme students Duncan and the late departed June McIlroy on the cusp of a lively riposte.

References

Brady, E.M., Cardale, A. and Neidy, J.C. (2013) 'The quest for community in Osher lifelong learning institutes', *Educational, Gerontology*, 39 (9), pp. 627–639.

Campaign to End Loneliness. (2014) Home page. Available at http://www.campaign-toendloneliness.org/ (Accessed: 26 December 2015).

Cattan, M., White, M., Bond, J. and Learmouth, A. (2005) 'Preventing social isolation and loneliness among older people: A systematic review of health promotion interventions', *Ageing and Society*, 25 (1), pp. 41–67.

Department for Work and Pensions. (2015) *2010 to 2015 government policy: Older people*, London: Department for Work and Pensions. Available at https://www.gov.uk/government/publications/2010-to-2015-government-policy-older-people (Accessed: 26 December 2015).

Field, J. (2005) *Social capital and lifelong learning*, Bristol: The Policy Press.

Findsen, B. (2005) *Learning later*, Malabar, FL: Kreiger Publishing Company.

Future Foundation. (2014) *The Future of loneliness: Facing the challenge of loneliness for older people in the UK, 2014–2030*, London: Future Foundation/Friends of the Elderly.

Glendenning, F. (1990) 'The emergence of educational gerontology', in Glendenning, F. and Percy, K. (eds.) *Ageing, education and society: Readings in educational gerontology*, Keele, Staffordshire: Association for Educational Gerontology, pp. 13–23.

Hallam, S. (2011) 'The role of participation in community music activities in promoting social engagement and well-being in older people', *NDA Findings 9* [online]. Available at http://www.newdynamics.group.shef.ac.uk/nda-findings-9.html (Accessed: 3 August 2015).

Local Government Association. (2012) *Ageing well: A whole system approach. A guide to place-based working*, London: Local Government Association. Available at http://www.local.gov.uk/c/document_library/get_file?uuid=8541bff1-fab7–413b-b2ef-d02ce743fcdb&groupId=10180 (Accessed: 26 December 2015).

Nechvoglod, N. and Beddie, F. (2010) 'Equality in VET: Good practice principles' [online]. Available at https://scholar.google.co.uk/scholar?cluster=111547670383 69655091&hl=en&as_sdt=0,5 (Accessed: 4 August 2014).

Office of the First Minister and Deputy First Minister. (2014) *Active ageing strategy: 2014–2020*, Belfast: Office of the First Minister and Deputy First Minister. Available at https://www.ofmdfmni.gov.uk/sites/default/files/consultations/ofmdfm_dev/active-ageing-strategy-2014–2020-consultation.pdf (Accessed: 26 December 2015).

Percy, K. (1990) 'Opinions, facts and hypotheses: Older adults and participation in learning activities in the United Kingdom', in Glendenning, F. and Percy, K. (eds.) *Ageing, education and society: Readings in educational gerontology*, Keele, Staffordshire: Association for Educational Gerontology, pp. 24–46.

UK Department of Health (2001) *National service framework for older people*, London: Department of Health.

Withnal, A. and Percy, K. (1994) *Good practice in the education and training of older adults*, Aldershot, Hants.: Ashgate Publishing Ltd.

World Health Organization. (2002) *Active ageing: A policy framework*, Geneva: World Health Organization.

Chapter 5

Reflections on the research process

As I have noted earlier, in the original research design of the project, we did not think about including some way of eliciting students' views about being involved in the research – what that process was like for them. Of course, it seems, looking back, that this was immensely short-sighted on my part, to say nothing of bearing a heavy enough burden of irony, for, in previous projects, I had been a great disciple altogether of the belief adumbrated by some experts in the field of qualitative research that an honest project's work should always build in what is called 'formative critical reflection', or to put it a bit more straightforwardly, that we should have the integrity to see our sins of commission and omission and then consider how we might make amends. It strikes me that this is not a million miles away from the wisdom of so many older people – that the process of becoming wise and making wise (sagacia-tion) has at its very core the optimistic and open-minded maxim that we can learn from our mistakes. So, realising that I had been hoisted rather upon my own petard, like Polonius in *Hamlet*, I then devised a questionnaire to 'cap-ture' this vital bit of 'data' – what is called by the experts 'meta-commentary' (Appendix 4). As far as I understand this term, it means that you include in the report of the research the reflections and responses of those who took part. To put this another way, a meta-commentary creates a way of talking about the process of the research itself, rather than simply recording the find-ings, and so allows us to go behind the findings to the people who have made the research, getting at their attitudes to it and thus learning how we might do things better in the future. And, most importantly, this meta-commentary becomes another way for learners to get their voice heard and to bring to bear their own wisdom to the project. Shortly, we will drill down into the detailed reflections of participants on the co-research process, but let us first take a look at the broader context, situating our researchers within the emerging fields of older people as co-researchers and students as co-researchers.

The broader context: student as co-researchers

The focus of this book is on older people who are students being actively involved as voicers, as co-researchers. The idea of actively involving the traditional 'subjects' of research in the design, development and actual implementation of the research is still by no means a universally accepted practice. The idea of engaging older people as active researchers is also fairly new (especially given the still prevailing 'construction' of older people as out of date, out of touch and a burden), and the idea of actively involving students as co-researchers within schools and universities is also fairly new. So, it is not surprising that there is even less expert academic opinion about the intersection of these domains: older students as researchers on their learning. It is our hope that this book will contribute to that intersection.

Reflections from the co-researchers: an overview

The importance of the learner voice: empowering the subject in research

Students testified to how important having a voice was. So, being able to give their views and listen to the often contrasting views of other students was adjudged to be a crucial outcome. I have spoken in the methodologies chapter about the 'reflective' turn and how this has caused academic researchers to think more deeply about how to include the 'subject' more equally in the research process. It might be said that, within the academic world, the notion that the 'subject' needs to have his or her own voice properly heard could be seen as a new intersection in terms of what we might plainly call 'attitude' across a number of different fields. This is what might be termed by academics a 'paradigm shift' – that is, a groundbreaking change in what is viewed as the purpose of research and, contingently, how it is conducted.

Older people as researchers

Many participants testified to their delight in being able to transfer knowledge they had gained earlier in their lives to this project. For older learners this was very ratifying. Some students also drew attention to how their participation as co-researchers challenged them to learn completely new skills. The old dog could learn new tricks, and older learners expressed their sense of delight in this discovery. Others focused on the new knowledge they had acquired, most especially about the broader context of ageing – the Big Picture. And others registered a sense of invigoration which, in a continuation of that questioning and critical stance which was often encouraged in the Open Learning classes, prompted them to challenge some of their own assumptions and received beliefs. That sense of suppleness, of not atrophying as older people into a set of rigid attitudes, that as older people they did not, in fact, know it all but had far more to learn, was there beneath the surface of the responses to many questions. Participants seemed rather delighted that they would resist comparison to T. S. Eliot's (1918) characterisation of Henry James, 'a mind so fine that no idea could violate it'.

The voices of older people in co-research are just beginning to be heard. Blair and Minkler (2009), for example, review 13 articles covering ten studies involving older people as researchers. They use participatory action research as their theoretical base – that is to say, the active inclusion of people affected by the issue being studied in the research and with the object of raising awareness, enhancing education and promoting social change. They comment that while such research is still rare, it has real potential both in helping understand complex issues more fully and in building individual and community capacity. In other words, older adults would be able to build on their new expertise to engage in further co-research. The article identifies a number of key issues for successful participatory action research, which include honouring the life experience of older people, building bidirectional trust and training with older adults.

Another article emanating from a social work context examined the perceptions of four groups on the involvement of co-researchers with dementia and from minority ethnic groups (Littlechild, Tanner and Hall, 2015). Co-researchers were trained and involved in the interviewing. The authors found that the co-researchers valued the process, thought they had contributed and felt validated. They gained knowledge, enhanced skills and developed networks and links to possible further involvement. They also benefited from the interaction with fellow co-researchers. The statutory organisation perspective was positive, quoting more colour in the information, and real information that might not otherwise have been uncovered. Voluntary organisations participating valued the intervention and were positive about the effect on individuals. Overall, the experts concluded there were benefits, both to the subjects and to the co-researchers, but concluded also that the method involves cost and time in training and managing the co-researchers and that such approaches work best for specific or local issues or situations rather than having a broader strategic focus. Both articles express concern about a possible lack of rigour and inadequate training. Littlechild *et al.* (2015) also raise an eyebrow about the ability of the researchers. I wonder if such a question would ever be raised about professional researchers. How would 'ability' be measured?

Gutman (2014) describes a project carried out in Israel in collaboration with a UK university. Older people were involved as co-researchers in the evaluation of a gerontological social work course, so there is an educational element here. The article reviews the general practice in social work of involving 'service users' in planning and delivering social work programmes. Gutman suggests that inclusion as co-students and co-teachers is well-established, but as co-researchers much less so. The new perspective is, they argue, to be welcomed. Participatory action research was also the research model used here. Older people were involved in interviewing and in the analysis of responses. Participants reported benefits in self-efficacy, empowerment and increased involvement in other university activities. And for the 'academy' the research benefited from their insight and input. Gutman argues for a process of critical reflection about alternative research paradigms, which might translate as discussing with the older adult participants different ways of looking at and tackling the research.

The article also rightly highlights the need to accommodate the needs and preferences of the older participants, including issues relating to health and availability. They also list the need for significant training input and explanations, and the need to cater for the older researchers' social and group needs. Overall, the conclusion is that there is a mutual benefit both to the research and to the older researchers, but there is a need for support, communication and involvement at all stages, including the project planning and the allocation of duties.

Walker (2007) has written about the involvement of older people in research within a health care context. He notes that funders now want explicit user involvement, but that some gerontologists are still sceptical since so little has been published on models of good practice. Older people are now asserting their right to be involved in policy, provision and research. As is reflected ahead in the discussion about students as researchers, Walker observes that there is a continuum between consumerism and empowerment (or perhaps a tension), but he notes that empowering older people as active research participants is still very rare; it is underfunded and time-consuming. But Walker is an advocate of the active involvement of older people, arguing that it is a human right, that it contributes to the quality of life of older people and that, as we hope to demonstrate ahead, it offers a challenge to negative stereotypes of older people through enabling them to represent themselves, to voice their reality. He refers to the New Dynamics of Ageing project as one example of good practice in having the first older people's reference group in a Research Council programme.

Students as co-researchers

Related to this was the emphasis which some participants placed upon being able to work as part of a team, made up from themselves as students and academics, to enquire into the perceptions of their fellow learners and to pool knowledge about the rich and varied wisdom of older learners. What do the experts say in relation to students as researchers? The consensus is that students are still mainly absent from research about their own teaching and learning, despite the fact that teaching and learning styles have a pretty direct impact on their experience as students (Trowler and Trowler, 2010; Boulton-Lewis and Tam, 2012; Healey, Flint and Harrington, 2014; Maunder, 2015). Maunder et al., in an earlier article (2013, p. 140) on a research project in which students played an active part in determining the interview questions and schedules, comment that a student-centred approach is condign in the current university climate, where students are viewed and view themselves as paying 'customers' or 'consumers'. As a result, she argues, students want more of a say in their education and their involvement has the potential to improve their experience of education.

Taylor and Wilding (2009, p. 4) use the term 'participatory pedagogy' to describe the idea of thinking about students as producers of knowledge rather than simply passive consumers, citing McCulloch (2009), and they view this new approach as an exciting and dynamic paradigm shift which also breaks down traditional barriers between teaching and research and between students and teachers. The University of Lincoln has also developed an initiative to challenge the traditional power imbalance between teacher and student and to strengthen student voicing. Bishop *et al.* (undated) usefully surveyed the increasing literature which is placing more emphasis on 'the learner voice as a way of enhancing learning and increasing learner engagement', arguing also for action research projects. Bishop, citing Gvaramadze (2011), rightly critiques the validity of more passive instruments for collecting student feedback, such as student satisfaction surveys.

At the University of Warwick and at Oxford Brookes University, for example, the Reinvention Centre for Undergraduate research proposes that positioning undergraduates as researchers challenges the hierarchical binaries between teaching and research, teachers and students. Taylor and Wilding (2009, p. 2) note that in the current environment of research-led institutions, students may be unaware of this culture in the absence of activities to engage them. The Reinvention Centre has, for instance, assembled a collaborative research team of undergraduate, postgraduate, postdoctoral and academic researchers and has even established a journal dedicated to the publication of high-quality undergraduate research. The University of Hertfordshire has also conducted student-staff collaborative research on student employability skills and the importance of trust being built between teachers and students is highlighted (Jarvis, Dickerson and Stockwell, 2013, p. 223).

Bishop *et al.* (undated) recommend that students be much more fully involved in the various levels of decision making about, for example, curricula and assessment, and also, interestingly, advocate the use of action research projects. Citing Coates (2005), they argue that there is a challenge in reconciling the constructivist perspective underpinning the idea of student engagement with what is ultimately an institutional responsibility for managing ongoing improvement. I would add, in relation to the projects that I have been involved with, that the constructivist perspective or conceptualisation of best practice teaching leads logically to the construction of co-learning and co-research projects which enable further empowerment for the learner, more imaginative and far-reaching articulation of the student voice and more imaginative teaching and learning. Gapp and Fisher (2006) critique the commonly used tool of student evaluations, arguing that students must be engaged in a deeper way, in their case through focus groups and discussions. They maintain that students who are truly engaged and involved can help to bring about change, but that a foundation of trust needs first to be built in order to persuade students to engage. So the institution needs to be viewed as supportive and encouraging in the first place in order to get students to participate.

Fielding (2001) has also spoken about the importance of student empowerment through active participation in research. This project involved three years of research projects between students and staff. All were trained in research, and in each year change was brought about through a dialogue between students and teachers. One interesting feature of this project was that students from the first year helped mentor students in the second year, a model I have used in education-in-the-community projects before now (Maginess, 2011) and which has potential for follow-on research. We will return to this in the conclusions and recommendations chapter. Fielding identifies different levels of engagement between learner and teacher, learners as a source of data, as active respondents, as co-researchers and as researchers. It would seem as if, in this project, we have got to the third level and that there is great potential for the fourth level. We will look at this in the conclusions and recommendations chapter.

Similar arguments about the benefits of student participation are reflected in reports from practice in schools. Writing from an Australian perspective, a student, Kallas (2011, pp. 19–20), argues that a 'respectful student-teacher partnership . . . improves the level of wellbeing and provides a sense of safety and belonging', noting also that students' thoughts and opinions are validated and considered'.

I would argue that by embedding the valorisation of the learner voice, respecting the student as co-producer of knowledge and skills, the foundation is laid for developing an organic form of research which arises naturally from pedagogic practice. Thus the not uncommon tension between academic research – and for the matter of that, student research – and teaching and learning can be reconciled. And, if the starting point is the question, 'what benefit is this pedagogy, this research to anybody – inside the university, beyond the university?', then we might be more likely to get the makings of a virtuous circle.

Finally, the making of tangible learning outputs – films, plays, books – especially involving interdisciplinary and creative approaches offers, I believe, further potential for students and teachers to see their learning and research as having meaning and substance. If such outputs can, in turn, influence policy or develop understanding and compassion around difficult topics, beyond as well as within academia, then universities may begin to be seen as dynamic contributors to society, not just in the rightly prized great medical and technological advances but also in a wide variety of disciplines which can benefit communities and societies. It may be noted that Blair and

Minkler (2009) specifically advocate the use of 'photovoice' methods, where photographic or video material enhances verbal records.

Research that contributes to society

Many respondents underlined the importance for them of being involved in a 'worthwhile' project, work that would be of some benefit to other older learners and to older people not currently engaged in education. Participants frequently emphasised their hope that the work they had done would have a positive benefit, encouraging older people to get involved, creating greater access for older people who were on low income or who were a bit daunted by the prospect of going back to education and influencing policymakers to consider how to make it easier for older people to participate because getting involved – under the right conditions – would enhance their wellbeing. Blair and Minkler (2009), however, realistically acknowledge that even small, incremental change is change that might well not otherwise have happened. Older people have the wisdom to know that they might not be able to change the world, but the conviction, nonetheless, is evidenced in the reflections of our participants that they might be able to change the world for the better a tiny bit.

Reflections from co-researchers: the detailed picture

Let us look now in more detail at what the participants have to say about their experience of the project. As is the way of all such matters, not all those who were involved responded. Those who filled in the questionnaire included interviewees and interviewers, a member of the steering group, a participant in one of the special courses and a student who contributed to the literature review and data analysis and one of the creative documenters. Here are their responses to the questions.

Motivation: why get involved in a co-research project?

One student, who participated also in one of the special projects, noted that he had 'always enjoyed studying, so another lifelong learning course seemed a natural progression from my university and teaching days'. This reflects a recurring theme in the findings: the sense of the Open Learning Programme as a natural continuation of a process of learning and studying.

Some students were prompted to participate because of what we might call an altruistic motivation. One stated, 'I wished to offer support (however small) for the project, which I envisioned would be a well worthwhile endeavour.' Another said, 'Because I believe in the objectives of the project'.

We may remind ourselves what the main objectives were: to investigate whether participation in the Open Learning Programme enhanced the wellbeing of older learners and to challenge negative stereotyping of older people. Another student's response is, I think, related but expressed more subjectively: 'I thought it would be very interesting to take part in this project, as its subject matter personally interests me very much, both in theory and practice.' This response turns up one side of the coin that we have seen in the findings: an *identification* with being an older learner. The other side of the coin is, of course, a kind of resistance to any labelling as an older person or older learner. One student said that he had got involved because he 'wanted to do something useful with his time'. This reflects a wider desire among older people to contribute to society and to have a sense of purpose.

Another student responded that the participation was motivated by the desire to learn new skills, 'to gain valuable experience in interview techniques'. What is salient here is that the student implies that interviewing techniques are for her or him a *new* skill. This goes back to McClusky's passionate assertion that the old dog can learn new tricks (McClusky, 1971, p. 416). And what is also salient is the use of that word 'valuable'; the student implies that new skills can be of use, that she or he can use these new skills in the world outside academia, whether that be to gain employment or to contribute as a volunteer. So the sense of older people being able to learn new skills and being able to activate their skills in society is a very powerful positive conviction about the potential for the contribution of older people, however quietly expressed.

One student, very movingly, said that he or she 'agreed to be involved to help older learners who might have been unsure about beginning or re-entering learning'. We have seen in the findings chapter that many of the learners were keen to spread the message of the benefits of participating in learning for older people and a recognition also, reflected so poignantly here, that many older people would, indeed, be unsure about beginning or re-entering learning. It is clear that this student saw the dissemination of the findings as a way of encouraging older people not currently involved in adult education or learning to be reassured and encouraged into it. The idea of being involved with something that had a purpose was also expressed by another student who said, 'The topic sounded interesting, and I wanted to do something useful with my time.'

First impressions: what gains might older learners expect?

One learner honestly responded that she or he had no clear idea of what might be gained from the project. One student responded that he wanted to 'learn and exchange ideas about the experience of old age and retirement'. The idea of learning as a gain in itself is noteworthy as is the belief that the project would be a forum for exchanging ideas and hearing the views of other learners. The aspiration to exchange ideas was also expressed by another respondent: 'I thought I would get the opportunity to work with others perhaps on interviewing, analysing interview summaries and on doing some basic computer charting.' Learning a specific skill was also the motivation for another student, stating that it was the 'experience in conducting interviews, including technique, tips and hints and how not to do it' which was her goal.

Thus, while one learner wanted to learn new skills, another saw the project as a vehicle for enacting skills and knowledge she or he already had, 'the satisfaction of exercising both my previous professional skills from the workplace, and using my acquired life skills constructively, too'. This registers beautifully a theme we have seen articulated many times in the findings: that older people, far from being burdensome and decrepit, have skills and knowledge and are keen to 'exercise' them. The same student added, 'also the knowledge that a high-quality defined result would be produced as a result of our trained team commitment'. I think what this shows is that learners do not want to sign up for just any old project; they want to identify themselves with work that they have faith in, that is goal-oriented and that promises a high-quality result. It is significant that this student also expected to receive training – to gain additional knowledge and skills — and also that he or she would be working as part of a team. And in a not dissimilar vein, another student expected to gain the 'satisfaction of seeing an important piece of research completed'. It is clear that students want to get older learners' views beyond the Open Learning Programme itself, beyond academia, on to the broader public agenda.

The student who was a creative documenter of the project said,

> I am interested in seeing people from an older age group getting so much out of adult learning. It is really important to many in the classes. Personally, I enjoy capturing images of subjects in a natural way, not posed and hopefully forgetting the camera. I hope the photographs will reflect how the students are engaged and enjoying their time in class.

First impressions: what might older learners expect to give to the project?

We then approached the issue of expectations from the other end of the telescope. While the wording admittedly lacks the magisterial rhetorical challenge of J. F. Kennedy's inaugural address (Kennedy, 1961), the intention was to draw out among the learners their sense of their own worth and wisdom, as well as discerning whether they felt that participation in a project like this did also have a kind of civic 'good', representing a form of public service to other people and to society more broadly.

One student thought that she or he 'might be able to contribute some ideas and personal anecdotes to illustrate my experience of Life Long Learning'. This student foregrounds both ideas – intellectual reflection – and personal anecdotes. It is an interesting response, in that the learner identifies two kinds of research approaches: one based more on intellectual reflection, perhaps extending to the formulation of theory or models, and the other based on what has been described as biographical or life history research. Indeed as is evident, the Sagaciation project encompasses both these approaches: drawing on the academic experts but enabling students to derive their own ideal model of lifelong learning and also grounding the research in the stories and personal anecdotes told by the learners.

Another student said, 'My time, energy, enthusiasm and effort'. The response quietly challenges negative stereotypes of older people. It is clearly not just the young who have this combination of qualities. Another student specifically focused on the unique contribution that older people make: 'a little bit of wisdom accumulated over 76 years'. Though the expression is modest, there is a terrific sense here of the latent potential of older people. This was echoed in another response: 'life experience which includes three university degrees'. The recognition that older people could draw upon existing skills was echoed by another respondent: 'I thought my old interviewing experience and my data presentation skills would be useful – as one of a large team.' And another response indicated a heartening confidence among older people that they do have skills and are very much in command of their marbles: 'a clear and enquiring mind and task focus, and a personal commitment to the project objectives'. Evident also in this response is that goal orientation we saw earlier and also the sense of faith in the aims of the project.

A creative documenter stated, 'I hoped to record images of what goes on in class, without disrupting the classes or posing the subjects. I hoped to be accepted, trusted and to blend in.' It is striking that the documenter was keen to build relationships of trust through her participation in the research, that the research should not be an alien and artificial business imposed upon students but a more organic and shared process.

Lasting impressions: reflecting on the actual experience of what co-researchers gained and gave

A majority of respondents said that their expectations of what they would both gain and give were fulfilled. One student, who attended one of the special classes and also was an interviewee, registered some bemusement: 'I wasn't sure what involvement meant.' Perhaps the literature for the project and my explanation of it to students should have made more explicit that attending the special courses was definitely a form of participation. There are lessons here for the future in terms of being really crystalline in explaining the project.

Four students said that their expectations had been met. The student who worked on the literature review and data analysis stated, 'My involvement was greater, more enjoyable, and more time-consuming than I expected. Rather than the data analysis and charting, literature review became the big issue for me.' And another student had this to say: 'Yes, although I thought there would be more training given'. So, expectations were mostly fulfilled with one student ending up becoming much more involved and another perhaps disappointed that more training had not been given. This was a difficult question for the project facilitators; it was, as one of the respondents stated with such clarity, vital that students would receive training, but on the other hand, the students were volunteers and the scale of the project fairly small, so we were reluctant to burden them with a commitment much beyond an afternoon. As it transpired, because older people are busy, we offered a second training session for those who could not attend the first. And, as noted in the methodologies chapter, students were also given the option of having a 'mentor' as they conducted their first interview. Here is what one interviewee said: 'I had presumed that the interview would have followed a more structured style of enquiry, but in fact the engagement of the interviewer made for a more interesting and enjoyable experience.'

Precious time: how much time would co-researchers spend on a small-scale research project?

Not surprisingly, the amount of time students committed was very varied, and that accords with the original intention: that learners could decide for themselves how much commitment they would give. We may remind ourselves, in terms of the scale of the project, that in addition to those involved in interviewing, other students did give up their time to assist in organising the scheduling, and others participated by enrolling in the special courses. This commitment would have varied from about four hours to about ten hours.

Here is a summary of responses:

- Three people reported a half-day, or a few hours.
- Four people reported a variety of inputs (e.g. 10 hours; 15–20 hours; six sessions; attending the classes) which might be described as moderate time contribution.
- One person reported approximately 24 days.

Some students spent 'one morning' on the project or 'a few hours'. Another 'conducted three interviews which took 20 minutes approximately, with two hours travelling time, and transcribed two which took one evening each'. And another detailed her involvement as follows: 'my initial one-to-one with the project director to ascertain my specific project interests, subsequently two afternoon group meetings, an interviewee session and two mornings as interviewer'. This response indicates a not uncommon feature – some students participated as both interviewees and interviewers.

The student who undertook to work on the literature review and the data analysis said, 'I don't honestly know! I think roughly a day per week for about 24 weeks – but that varied enormously.' I may note that this student gave a tremendous amount of time to the project. One of the creative documenters said that she spent 15–20 hours on the project.

Training for and with co-researchers: how much training, what kinds of training?

As noted in earlier chapters, training was offered by project facilitators to those who wished to become interviewers, and the student who wished to work on the literature review was also offered training by the School of Education librarian.

One student reported that he or she 'received guidance from Tess which was useful and one talk beforehand on the creation of the interview questions which I did not find particularly useful'. While the less than entirely favourable response might sting a little, it is ratifying to know that students felt they could be honest, for that is the only way we can make amends. In future projects, I would review the questionnaire aspect of the training and go back to this student for advice on how it might be done better. Another student recognised that 'training was essential within the parameters of the project to guarantee its validity, and so very useful'. This student added, 'It was very good that we all had the chance in group session to comment on the draft questions and suggest amendments.' Blair and Minkler (2009) stress that involvement in discussion about interview questions is as important as being involved in conducting the interviews. The student who received training from the librarian found it very worthwhile, allowing him to understand much better what academic research entailed.

While, as we have seen earlier, academics commenting on research with older people rightly emphasise the importance of training, it is also important to strike a balance between what students would definitely need to know and not encroaching too much on their time. The reflections from the students on training are somewhat inconclusive, so I am not sure if we got the balance right or whether we should have offered more training or training that was perhaps more focused on some of the practical challenges of interviewing – and indeed, being interviewed. However, it must be said that the interviews were very successful in capturing a lot of rich data, so perhaps the short training sessions and the mentoring were adequate for the scale of the project. Upon reflection, for future projects, while it is not common practice, I would also offer training to interviewees; after all, that is a bit of a strange and new experience.

Co-research as a vehicle for drawing on and exercising existing skills and knowledge?

Here is a summary of responses to this question:

- Yes – 8. This was the most straightforward and emphatic 'yes'.
- Using previous experience of interviewing.
- Experience of relating to people when entering a group.
- Establishing rapport with other students.

This question was aimed at drawing out from the participants some reflections on how older learners are able to use the experience and knowledge they already have – their sagacity, in a new context. To put this another way, whether skills and knowledge are 'transferable'. All respondents agreed that this was the case. Some students simply answered 'yes'. One added, 'And this was most satisfying and fulfilling for me'. This is, I think, very telling. Without wishing to read too much into this answer, I would suggest that the student considered the opportunity to draw on extant skills and knowledge satisfying was because he or she experienced a kind of ratification of knowledge and skills that were not always called upon or valued. People like to be invited to offer their expertise. Wanting to feel valued is a fundamental human need.

One student drilled down into the question by responding that 'Yes – it was reassuring to find I could still think! Searching libraries and following themes in literature was refreshing and personally reassuring.' Thus, participation in the project was a way of reassuring older people that they did have skills and knowledge and that they were still capable of exercising these skills.

For other students, the sense of validation was derived from being able to revive specific skills and knowledge. One student stated that she or he was able to use past experience of one-to-one consultations for interviewing, while another learner found it helpful to be able to draw on 'previous experience of interviews in research for my dissertations'. For another student, experience as a teacher gave her greater confidence in conducting interviews: 'Yes, my previous experience was helpful in allowing me to enter a class or group without too much reluctance.' And for one of the creative documenters, both technical and people skills were vital: 'I have always had to strike up a very quick rapport and trust with my subjects. If I can't do this, I can't get the shots.'

Co-research as a vehicle for developing new skills and knowledge?

The great majority of respondents said that they had acquired new skills and knowledge. Two students honestly responded that they had not learned any new skills or knowledge. While the ideal would have been for participants to gain new knowledge and skills, I think it is also important to acknowledge that not all will. Perhaps it is good enough that older learners consolidate and transfer the skills they already have within a research process. However, the other respondents all said that they had learned new skills and knowledge. One simply said yes, but did not specify. Another answered that he or she 'enjoyed very much hearing other very different views in the learning process'. This is an interesting response, implying that one of the dimensions of Open Learning classes which learners appreciated – the chance to hear different points of view – was present also in the interview process. So an exchange of learning did take place for this student. Another student echoed this aspect: 'I polished and kept current old skills and was very interested to learn of the very different reactions and appreciations to their courses, of my three very different in personality type, assigned interviewees.'

For the student who worked on the literature review and the analysis of the data, participation in the research enabled him to learn 'how to use modern computerised library databases and catalogues, along with how to list references properly. I also learned an enormous amount about ageing, about attitudes to ageing, and about the factors that contribute to "healthy ageing" and wellbeing'. It is significant that this student was able to gain a very broad picture of the topic and to relate direct experience to what the experts were saying, thus being able to link practice and theory. I would deduce from this that in future projects I would encourage more students to engage with this side of the research.

One student framed the answer within a broader context of older people's capacity and enthusiasm for learning:

> We are always learning. There is much to be gained every day. I have the utmost respect for those who can open our minds to new experiences and for those who are so generous with their knowledge and experience. Our mature friends and acquaintances have so much to offer.

Is getting involved in co-research challenging for older learners? If so, how?

Some students responded that their involvement in the project had not challenged them. Again, while the ideal would have been for learners to have been 'stretched' a bit, I think these responses could be read as an indication of the confidence of some older learners in their own experience and skills. One respondent commented that being challenged had been a positive experience, suggesting that people gain greater benefit from things that are a challenge than from those that are comfortable.

One participant stated that the project was challenging 'to a minor degree, just by having to concentrate my mind on the exact nature of my thoughts and feelings in relation to ongoing personal development during retirement'. I would submit that the student is understating rather the importance of the challenge she or he articulates, for, as we have seen in the findings chapter, many older learners have quite ambivalent responses to being classified as older learners. So, if this student was encouraged by the project to really think about a topic and a positioning that has about it a certain difficult air, then that to me is a profound challenge. If the project created the conditions for even one participant embarking on a self-reflection not just about courses or teaching styles but about negotiating identity – what it means to be now an older learner, an older person – then perhaps that is an index of success.

One student responded, 'No, I felt I was both practising my formerly acquired skills' but then went on to say,

> and also learning of the very varied and interesting reactions of older learners who had attended the same class, but took different interpretations and reactions to it, both according to their personality type and their own previous work and learning experiences.

Implicit here is the idea that the respondent did find it challenging to hear interpretations and reactions to the programme that differed from her or his own. Again, we hear reiterated an honest admission that others do have different views and, far more importantly, an openness among students to attend to contrasting, even contradictory points of view. This was echoed in the response of another student who said she or he did the find the project challenging: 'Yes, in terms of nature of individuals and how to deal with their varying personalities'. This response brings out another aspect of the research process itself – how do participants cope not just with points of view different from their own, but with different sorts of personalities? When arranging the interview schedule, I deliberately adopted a random 'pairing' process, going by alphabetical order. This was quite deliberate as I was aware that some of the students knew each other and I wanted to avoid cosy set of pairings which would see friends or students with similar outlooks and personalities interviewing one another. And, of course, as we have noted in the methodologies chapter, the very form of the interaction, the more than slightly artificial mode of communication that is the academic 'interview' creates a kind of odd distancing, and people speak about a situation that they are all familiar with in a rather different way. We must remember that the 'interview' in a research project is a construct created by academics and reporters and that people do not naturally interact with one another in an interview mode.

And there is another issue; if interviewer and interviewee know each other, then one or another may interrupt the objective flow of question and answer by 'breaking their lines', if not to weep, or even laugh, then to offer some commentary, criticism or advice. There is a wonderful documentation of this in a project which took place in the Netherlands involving older people. A voluntary interviewer discovers that he knows the lady he is interviewing, and there is mutual delight. They start to talk about how they might be related (going off at a tangent from the questions) and when the lady begins to describe her financial situation, he goes off at another tangent, advising her how she might access certain benefits (Bindels *et al.*, 2014). The academics involved were rather disapproving of this. Now I have to say that while I quite see the sincere desire to maintain academic objectivity and rigour, I would be disinclined to censure such a turn of events. To me, the discovery that interviewer and interviewee might be kinsfolk could help build trust in what was, for both parties, an artificial situation, and if one party can learn something relevant and helpful to their real life, surely that is not so bad a thing? This raises the very huge question of whose agenda is it? If we are to genuinely engage in co-research, the participants as well as the academics need to be in charge of the content and the process. This echoes the argument made very eloquently by Messiou (2013) in her article on working with students as co-researchers in schools, where she stresses the importance of inclusivity: that the academic researcher/teacher should be careful not to dominate the process but to facilitate students to develop skills and criticality.

In this particular project, students sat on the steering group and so were empowered to refine or even radically alter the focus and methods of the research. Students were invited to participate in whatever way they deemed interesting, and those who kindly volunteered to be interviewers had the opportunity to throw out questions or substitute them.

In relation to the conduct of the interviews, considering that many of the students did know one another or were, at least, part of a common cohort as fellow students in the Open Learning Programme, I felt that a little bit of distancing and artifice was actually helpful in avoiding a too superficial consensus or a set of bland responses from what we might term the 'body of the Kirk'. That some interviewers struggled a bit, myself included, in repositioning from friend, acquaintance or vaguely familiar fellow student there is no doubt. None of us were professional interviewers (or indeed, professional interviewees), and even with a bit of training, the actual experience of two people sitting face to face with one person firing, however gently, a set of questions and the other trying to think on the spot of answers is a bit intimidating.

And the young master's students as interviewers had to overcome another little 'unlocal' difficulty; they were not used to interviewing people and were not studying topics which focused on older people. It is a tribute to the students, young and old, that there were no disasters.

In relation to challenges, one student wittily noted, 'In my own working life surveys, I had to analyse my results and write a report, so just doing the interviewing without having to analyse it was a decided treat!' I can only hope that our analysis measures up to her or his expertise.

Another student responded to the question like this:

> It challenged my confidence at first, as I hadn't done anything similar for years, but Tess encouraged me and gave me confidence that I actually could do something useful. It fits in with the research – that we get the greatest benefit from things that are a challenge rather than comfortable and easy.

For another, participation in the special courses represented a welcome challenge to continue on a journey of learning: 'Yes, it encouraged me to read more and to continue taking other lifelong learning courses.'

One of the creative documenters candidly acknowledged some of the technical and logistical issues of taking photographs across a number of venues, working alongside a film crew, smallish spaces and lighting that was not always ideal. Of course, bringing in spotlights might have mitigated this, but would have been more intrusive; or we could have done all the photography in one or two more photogenic rooms, but this would have created a sort of 'here's one we prepared earlier' quality, spawning suspicion of 'spin' and would also have caused a lot of disruption to the students as we shunted them from their normal teaching rooms or called them in specially for their 'photo/film shoot'. So there is always a balance, and for us the most important criteria were to document the project in the most unobtrusive way possible so that students were at their ease. The photographer, it must be said, displayed great patience as well as resourcefulness in dealing with the limitations she was faced with. The filmmakers were equally low-key, and one said to me afterwards that he had become totally absorbed in the workshop session on *King Lear*, saying he had never really 'got' Shakespeare before! So some unexpected learning also took place.

What's not to like about being engaged with co-research? Was there any aspect of your involvement that you did not enjoy?

All respondents except one stated that there was no aspect of the process that they did not enjoy. That student questioned whether his or her views had been accurately recorded. One student noted, 'I appreciated the optional choice re using a recording device. If this had been mandatory I would have disliked it intensely!' We did consider this quite carefully in advance, being aware that some older learners might find the prospect of being recorded intrusive or likely to make them self-conscious. As noted earlier in the methodologies chapter, younger interviewers would tend to use a digital recorder almost as a default mode, whereas the older interviewers, conditioned to making handwritten notes in lectures or other such formal situations, would have tended to use this mode of recording the interviews. In my own case, being of the older generation and thus pretty quick at making notes in tempo with speech, I used this method, but backed it up with digital recording when interviewees were agreeable. It must be said that there are some advantages of using a digital recorder because it allows the interviewer to free himself or herself into a more interactive relationship with the interviewee. The disadvantage is, ironically, that the interviewee may feel that they must be more circumspect and formal since everything they say is being recorded.

In an effort to create trust and reassurance between interviewer and interviewee, we established it as a principle of the interviewing process that the interviewee would have an opportunity to read the transcript and to correct any inaccuracies or to omit or add to the script. All students, including the one who expressed some worry that she or he would not be accurately recorded, did have the chance to read the transcript. Some interviewees did suggest minor amendments and these were incorporated. I acknowledge that this is not always normal practice in academic interviewing, but my view is that it is crucial to have this checking mechanism; in the first place, the interviewee or, as it is called in academic research, the 'subject' has, in most cases, given voluntarily of their time and expertise and thus should be accorded the courtesy of seeing the transcript before it is taken into an academic realm over which they have no control. This kind of research would not be possible without the active participation of the interviewees, and it seems to me that if we are to be true to the spirit of co-research, the interviewee must be empowered to challenge and amend what they themselves are reported to have said and also to add and expand what might, upon reading it back, have seemed cryptic or unclear, or not quite right. The interviewer has nothing to lose from this except a small bit of pride – the sense that they have not quite got it right. But, then, so often the theme of challenge has recurred in this project, and I think our participants were not wholly on the side of Lady Violet in *Downton Abbey*, who quipped, with regard to her dispute with her nemesis, Mrs Crawley, that opponents are perfectly entitled to disagree as long as they do not win the argument.

Looking at the matter from a more academic point of view, as we have seen in the methodologies chapter, professional, academic interviewers are abjured to establish validity and reliability. And one obvious way of doing this is to check back with the interviewee. We are all guilty of hearing selectively, of being nervous and not catching all that is said, or not hearing accurately, or getting split between listening and recording. One example is in an interview I conducted with a most delightful and enthusiastic interviewee, and she compared coming to the Open Learning classes to 'opening a bottle of Cordin [something]'. Alas, in this case, as interviewer, I was not, as the interviewee was, at all well-up on fine French wine and so completely missed the analogy. I sent the transcript back to her with apologies for my *gaucherie* and received in return not only the proper spelling of the wine but also some delightful additional comments.

Far be it from me to challenge the established norms of academic interview practice, but it does seem that, in the spirit of co-research and, well apart from that, in the interests of 'capturing' more rigorous data, the idea of checking back with the 'subject' might be worthy of some slight consideration.

Does co-research provide a means of developing networks?

This question was grounded in my awareness that, for some students, the social dimension of the Open Learning Programme was important to them, and I was interested to discover whether participation in the research about the programme would, in itself, engender friendships or networks. More than half the respondents said that they had not really developed new networks or friendships through the research.

While it would have been delightful if participants had established friendships or networks through participation, I have to acknowledge that this would have been an unexpected bonus; interviewers and interviewees were brought together for short periods of time and perhaps the constraints of a semi-formal and somewhat artificial situation did not lend itself to the striking up of friendships. Perhaps a longer period of interaction might have produced this, or perhaps as project facilitator, I should have been less strict about the time allocated or even the scope of the interview. However, I was conscious that participants were giving their time voluntarily and were also, to some extent, in arranged marriages between interviewers and interviewees; love or even friendship or even 'nice acquaintance' does not always blossom under such hothouse conditions. And I must again reflect that a calling together of participants after the interviews might have helped to enforce greater group or team solidarity and developed a better sense of the co-research ethos of the project.

One student noted that participation in the project, through enrolling in one of the special courses, did enable him to 're-establish networks with teaching colleagues'. And one student commented, 'Yes – both with Tess and with other members of the QUB [Queen's University, Belfast] class. I look forward to continuing to be involved.' One student did form new friendships: 'Yes, really interesting new friends'.

What are the views of co-researchers about older learners and older people as a result of reflecting on their experience?

This question provoked the greatest volume of comment. All but one participant reported a variety of positive learning, either personal or more generally about older learners. The one exception cautiously reported that they had not yet learned anything, but may do when the findings are published. In a moving and lyrical tribute to how participation in the project and in the programme more generally enhanced her wellbeing, one student said,

> It reinforced for me my own attitude to life; Louis MacNeice's 'the drunkenness of things' being various. It reinforced for me how varied in personalities and interests we older people are, and how we all bring our former working and personal lives to bear on new learning scenarios.

Another student echoed this very buoyant attitude to being an older learner:

> having to collect my thoughts together and articulate them in the interview scenario helped reiterate for me my positive approach and appreciation

of the advantages of being able to avail of Queen's Lifelong Learning Programme. I cannot say that that my views of older learners or people have altered.

It is evident that for this student the project afforded an opportunity to stand back from her learning and to voice her views. It is encouraging that reflection on the programme has confirmed a very supportive view of Open Learning and at a deeper level how the programme and her participation in the project have served to confirm her own positive approach to being an older learner. This was echoed by another response:

> about myself: I learned that I still enjoyed getting engrossed in a topic, that I could still scan and summarise academic papers, and that I had something to offer. About older learners, many, many things – many cheering and optimistic things about our continued ability to learn, the contribution we can make to the 'Mental Capital' of the community, and the benefits to our wellbeing (emotional, mental and physical) from being involved in continuing education.

But it must be said that not all older learners had quite so spry a view of becoming older: 'old age is no joke which I always have expected to be the case.'

For another student, the chance to 'articulate what I felt about learning' was the main learning outcome. This reinforces the idea that older people really do appreciate having their voices heard, being empowered to comment critically and at length about the programme they participate in, rather than being merely passive consumers. Another student took a rather different approach, emphasising the value of the intergenerational aspect of the programme: 'there are some really good courses being held and that it's not just old people that do them'. Another learner emphasised the benefits of a shared learning process: 'I enjoyed meeting people. I realise that we will always benefit from both learning new things and sharing our knowledge with others throughout our lives. We have much to be gained through a good shared learning scheme.'

One student remained unconvinced that he or she had learned anything significant: 'but I might, from the findings of the research, once they are published'. Hope springs eternal. This last comment does reflect, however, another aspect of the research process. While the learners were part of a team and gained a sense of this from the training sessions, nonetheless they were mostly operating 'solo missions' in the actual conduct of the research. And, as a result, they were not really aware of the 'results' from their fellow students. If I was doing the project again, I would hold a briefing session with participants, or send them a preliminary report of the findings. When the book is published, I would very much welcome the opportunity to bring all the participants together to celebrate, to thank them with a bite to eat and a drink or a cup of tea. It is my intention also that all participants will receive a free copy of the book. So, there are lessons here about keeping participants, as well as the steering group, briefed throughout. Had they had access to the preliminary findings, this may have inflected their responses to the questionnaire, as they would have been more aware of what their fellow learners had discovered. And the responses may well have been fuller or more reflective.

Can participation in co-research enhance wellbeing and wisdom? If so, how?

Most respondents thought that it could. Two respondents candidly answered 'no' and a third, 'not really'. Again, though not the answer I would have hoped for, I am grateful to the students for their honesty and it is a mark of the trust built during the project. It would be worth returning to these students to try to gain their suggestions about how the project could have been improved or if there would be another kind of project which might fulfil this objective.

One student offered this beautifully stoical response: 'Yes, "The young doth rise where the old doth fall." Ageing is a natural process for us all, and so learn to accept it and be thankful for what you have had.' In contrast, another student stated, 'This was a feel-good project!'

This is echoed by another learner: 'Yes, it gave me a sense of achievement and I enjoyed the praise of the interviewee, who stated that I transcribed his words exactly right.' So, this participant was borne up by the ratification offered by another student, and the sense of a job well done.

One participant offered a very extensive reflection on how the project had enhanced her wellbeing:

> Very much so. I was able to re-visit and use again my previous work skills and am very pleased they still up to scratch! Good for self-esteem and confidence. I enjoy taking on projects such as this, in areas of personal interest, with defined beginnings, middles and ends – quite unlike the ongoing nature of my own professional life. I like engaging with people for a common constructive purpose and just at present – for a brief moment of time – I am actually in different areas, engaging with all the generations and I feel that each different generational involvement both enhances me personally, and also gives me new ways and insights for me to use in working with the other generations – e.g. the life wisdom and appreciation of these older learners contrasting with the enthusiasm but inexperience of the primary children I volunteer with helps me to communicate better with each end of life experience.

There are many themes adumbrated in this answer: the opportunity to use previous skills and to realise that she or he still had plenty of capacity. This echoes a common theme in the findings and indeed in what the experts say:

that older people possess a wealth of skills and that these skills do not disappear. Furthermore, the chance to exercise extant skills in a new context – or to transfer skills – creates wellbeing too, offering new platforms to older people.

The student also indicated that being part of a team, engaging with people for a common purpose, also enhanced wellbeing, again echoing another theme expressed in the findings and in the literature – that older people find working together in groups to be ratifying. And that sense of having a goal, a 'common purpose', is echoed by earlier comments in the reflections from the participants. And perhaps more saliently, there is also the preference for a project that has limits – beginnings, middles and endings. One of the anxieties which can arise from research projects is that the participants do not know what they are letting themselves in for and, as a result, may shy away from commitment. We must remember that it is not just younger people who often have busy lives. As stated earlier, it was made clear to participants that they had the power to decide what exactly they wanted to do in relation to this project and the time commitment was spelled out.

This student also touches upon another theme which occurs elsewhere in the reflections and also in the findings: the sense of wellbeing which can be derived from becoming involved in intergenerational projects; that older people, while they may wish to be with their peers in some respects, also welcome opportunities to engage with the coming generations, offering their life experience but also enjoying the enthusiasm of young people.

And here is another positive and detailed response, this time from the student who participated in the literature review and data analysis, Allen Young:

> Yes – I was really delighted to learn how to use the new library, and reassured by being able to contribute something apparently useful. It also put me in touch with a lot of writing and research about ageing that I would not otherwise have had access to. I now can talk more confidently to friends and family about the realities of ageing – both the harsh realities and also the positives. I find I argue more against people who trot out stereotypical comments about older people – frequently themselves – and put the more positive angle. I had always been aware of the issues of 'wellbeing' and contentment, and am armed with more research data about the factors that contribute to wellbeing in older people.

Here the student stresses his delight at learning new skills and shares his sense of enhanced wellbeing through being able to contribute something apparently useful. This idea of being able to contribute, to serve a public good, is evident also in the last student's comments. And we have noted earlier how older people often do express their desire to offer something to society, to look outwards beyond their own individual perspectives and to help others.

This student also derives a sense of wellbeing from gaining a much broader perspective on the topic of ageing through reading the literature on the subject. And, very movingly, this new knowledge is communicated to friends and family – making ageing a topic that, so to speak, can be talked about, frankly and in a balanced way. And talking about ageing, based upon a deeper knowledge through his reading, the student has become a quietly powerful voice too for challenging negative stereotypes of ageing. Significantly, the student acknowledges that older people themselves 'trot out' the stereotypes – internally colonising how the dominant forces in society choose to represent ageing. There has been a great deal of very powerful books and essays written by experts – including older people – challenging in often subtle and nuanced ways the idea that age must always be negative. As we have seen earlier, many of the experts talk about the 'cultural construction of ageing' – that is to say that our current society creates images of ageing that are frequently frightening, repulsive or inimical and even hostile. But, as I have noted before, the literature offers us many examples of how older people can resist these stereotypes and construct their own truth about the experience of ageing, just as years ago, disabled people began to challenge how they were viewed or constructed. At first they did it individually (often lone and marginalised voices), and then in groups of various kinds and then by getting their voice heard in policy and academic circles. So change can happen – we can shift those hegemonies. But the most powerful agents of change will be older people themselves.

Can being involved in co-research about older learners by older learners contribute to challenging negative stereotypes?

Two participants answered 'no', another 'maybe', one was unsure, two hoped that this would be the case and two said 'yes'. Nonetheless, the question was also designed to probe participants' views of how being involved in the project may have caused them to articulate their own personal challenge to negative stereotyping. The participants who said 'no' and the participants who were not sure may have produced this response out of a sense of modesty, or because they were simply had no objective way of knowing whether this might turn out to be the case. I acknowledge that the question was, in that sense, impossible to answer in advance of the dissemination of the results.

Of the students who answered, 'hopefully', one added, 'I do hope so. I hope that we can show that maturity = knowledge and valuable experience.' Again, this answer is tied implicitly to how the positive results of the research might gain traction in the outside world, among policymakers and in society generally.

Of those who said 'yes', one wryly noted, 'My friends, neighbours and family will ruefully agree.' It is clear from this response that the student has, through participation in the project, become a sort of advocate for the case that engaging in learning, and furthermore in research, can challenge negative stereotypes. The response also reveals that the case is not self-evident and must be made, and made intergenerationally – that is to say that older people need to be convinced by their peers that the prevailing negative hegemony can be challenged and that younger family members and friends also need to be persuaded that the 'crusties' still have something to learn from the young and something to say from their own experience that might benefit, might assuage and might develop resilience and, dare I say it, a kind of dignity among younger people.

It is interesting that the most positive answers came from those whose participation had been the greatest in terms of time and a more sustained engagement with the project, especially in terms of reading what the experts said about ageing and older learners.

Do co-research projects with older people have the potential to help other older people? If so, how?

All except one respondent answered in the affirmative. That student said, 'I will await until I see the results.' Others were more upbeat. One participant responded, 'This research project will undoubtedly add to the knowledge base from which older people will draw inspiration and encouragement to pursue and develop their own individual interests and talents into their third age.'

In their response to this question, learners had discovered, by articulating through the process of the research project, the many benefits of being involved in lifelong learning, and having come through that process, they had realised much more fully the benefits not just for themselves but also for other older people not currently involved. One student thought that the findings from the project would 'offer a sense of achievement, give them [the participants] a sense of purpose and broaden their circle of friends'. Other participants saw the project as a means through which other older people would learn about and get involved in adult education: 'I hope that it would encourage older people to become engaged with learning.' And another participant added, 'Yes, it's good to go to a class and meet people.'

Another learner was very definite about the myriad beneficial effects of the project in terms of discovering and articulating the positive impact of older people not just getting involved in education but also being reflective about that involvement:

> We live in a sensation-driven world of very immediate superficial contacts. Older people are often depicted as a problem, a nuisance, powerless. But reading the results of this factually-driven project should give

a sense of pride and positivity to older people and a clear sense of how they can use the luxury of the time they now have in their lives. It will also inform the younger generations of how best to engage with them positively. Also, I imagine that all the older people involved in this project feel as I do, that it has been very constructive on a personal level and good for their sense of community (of learners) involvement, self-esteem, and that we have been good role models for our peers.

The project – the gathering of evidence about what the learners actually think of the programme and feel about it – has, for this learner, raised much larger questions about how older people are currently represented and how participation in the courses offers a very different image or 'construction' of older people. A more salient aspect emerges also: older people have the time, at last, to think, to reflect, and this is liberating. Some older people, freed from a lifetime of having to govern their tongue and having to concentrate on professional or family imperatives, or juggling both, now can, at last, pursue their own path, go on their own journey.

The intergenerational dimension surfaces also: how participation in lifelong learning better equips older people to engage positively with young people. Again, we hear that enthusiasm, that understanding that older people need to be open to change, that the world is not what it was when they were young, that they can learn from younger people as well as showing them a trick or two.

And there is the sense that older people can act as role models, ambassadors, keepers of the flame, encouraging those not already involved, not through a top-down imperative but through peer endorsement.

Another student stressed the policy implications:

> Yes – I think the strength of the evidence that continuing education is a particularly valuable activity in maintaining a sense of wellbeing should influence policymakers and politicians in their planning and budget allocation. It should also encourage people who have not been involved to sign up and get involved. I think it demonstrates the value both of continuing education in general, and also the benefits of being involved in the research process.

For another student, the shared learning experience was very fulfilling: 'the environment is "safe" and conducive to joining in. This can only be good for self-esteem and wellbeing.'

Once more unto the breach? Can engagement in one co-research project encourage older learners to do further projects?

Almost all respondents said that they would be willing to undertake further projects. While it would be enormously satisfying to report that all participants were leaping at the chance to become involved in further projects, the truth is that, while no participants registered any negative experience of being involved, one participant candidly responded 'no'. Perhaps this is a little like Mr Bennet in *Pride and Prejudice*, who, having listened to his rather earnest daughter play a little laboriously for the company, tersely declared, 'Thank you, Mary, you have delighted us long enough.' Or maybe, the student, having participated – and without any great harm and having even enjoyed the experience – simply wants to move on to other interests, other passions. Life is, after all, short.

Another respondent said that she or he 'would probably be happy to be involved in a minor way'. This answer reflects a sense of delimitation; perhaps like the respondent earlier, the student has other priorities. In the findings chapter we have heard often expressed the delight among older people that they are at last free to make their own choices, to say yes and say no. So, the response may well denote a kind of liberation among older people, which is surely a cause for celebration. Or perhaps the student is simply being modest. If that is the case, maybe, as facilitator, I should have done more to value the contribution of each student, to build confidence and ratify participants more individually, more personally. While I did write to each, maybe I could have done more.

Other respondents indicated that they would be willing to engage in further research projects. Two said they would be very willing participants. One student playfully answered, 'Yes – probably in the same ways – but I am open to offers!' Another answered, with considerable gusto, 'Yes, please. I'd be happy to be involved in thinking, reading, writing, analysing. You name it.' There is no doubt that some participants definitely got the 'research bug'. That is an exciting and encouraging outcome.

Duck ponds or a wing and a prayer? Co-research and the issue of expenses/payment

Students were offered expenses, and this was made clear on the information flyer and in the training sessions, but it must be acknowledged that the message was not communicated clearly enough as two students said that they were not offered expenses. A couple of the students did claim expenses and were given them – notably, the younger master's students. Perhaps this reflects a somewhat different outlook among older learners, who saw their contribution as voluntary and as a form of public service, or perhaps they did not feel that they needed the extra money. Older people in Northern Ireland are entitled to free travel, so this may also have been a factor. As noted earlier, the project expenses were funded through my National Teaching Fellowship grant. A larger application for funding did not proceed because the funder had the particular scheme withdrawn due to a cut in their funding. This effectively meant that we were not able to employ professional researchers. However, since my own *modus operandi* had been, over many projects, to work with learners as co-researchers, this was not a major issue, and perhaps unreflectingly, I had proceeded on the same premise as the students themselves: that we were all giving a lot of time voluntarily. It must also be said that in previous co-research projects, external funding had been obtained to enable non-traditional learners to access the workshop-based learning and research projects for free and with funding built in for childcare, respite, transport and other support needs (Maginess, 2006).

Nonetheless, within mainstream higher education, the issue of whether student co-researchers should be incentivised in some way has been addressed by some academics. One student said, in response to a later question, that she or he would like to be involved in another project but 'as a fee-paid interviewer/transcriber'. While participants were offered expenses, they were not paid as 'professional' researchers. And this raises some very big questions about the whole basis of co-research projects between students and academics. I am aware that there are now, in higher education, pioneering schemes, like the University of Northampton's Undergraduate Bursaries Scheme, which offers students £500 each to participate in research projects which are related to the student learning experience. For cash-strapped students, £500 would, doubtless, be a great help and, by comparison with professional research rates, is pretty small (Maunder, 2015).

However, it may also be true that students and teachers should, in the long run, 'hardwire' these kinds of projects into their quality assurance and student experience satisfaction performance measures. But care needs to be taken that this very valuable work is not turned into as yet another kind of performance measurement for teachers nor an additional burden for students; so the current autonomy and opt-in principles need to be preserved to gain maximum commitment from both teachers and students.

There are a couple of ways of looking at this; on one hand, student co-researchers are, it must be frankly admitted, not, within the standards and values understood by academics, trained or experienced to the extent of, let us say, a postgraduate researcher, generally the 'level' within the academic world where a researcher might be considered professional. On the other hand, student co-researchers operating at undergraduate level, technically speaking, but bringing to the project a wealth of experience and skills as older people may well arguably be at this level in terms of the sophistication of their apprehension. Thus, the case could be made that experiential knowledge more than compensates for a lack of theoretical knowledge about research methodologies or other academic imperatives, and thus, within the larger framework of 'user research', co-researchers should be paid at equivalent market rates to professional researchers. This leads us into a much deeper debate about how the academy views research participants. The orthodox view has been that participants are, essentially, research 'subjects' who supply answers to questions posed by academics. In such a construction, payment to participants is rarely considered and indeed would be considered unethical as payment might be deemed to influence responses.

However, in a co-research project the power relationship and contingently the financial imbalance between academics and participants become much more 'exposed'. But then there is another sort of argument altogether; is research a commodity that must be traded? The reality is that professional researchers are paid professional rates and participants are not. Should participants, including 'subjects', be paid for their time and, indeed, their expertise, and at the same rate as the professional researcher? Or, as is reflected among many older learners, is participation in research a form of public good, a way of contributing to society? Some participants did not expect to be paid and did not want to be paid, to the point of indignation. These are profound questions for the academy in terms of how it considers its position in relation to what it considers the purpose and benefit of research.

Additional reflections on being co-researchers

The additional comments were all positive. Two learners noted that they really looking forward to seeing the finished product, and I think this reflects the sense, expressed earlier, that older learners value being involved in research which has a goal, a purpose and an end *product* or tangible outcome, that will 'get out there'.

Another learner focused more on the *process* of being involved in the research:

> I have gained a lot of positive benefit from the project, both in terms of my own knowledge of, and insight into, the issue of ageing (which is a very relevant one for me!) and in terms of my feeling of usefulness. It has enhanced my perception of the continuing education programmes I have been involved in, and encouraged me to do more. It also has made me an ambassador for the whole process. I'm sure people are tired listening to me trotting out the latest useful bit of research I've read, or today's positive snippet about the realities of ageing, and ranting against the stereotypical view of the old as a burden on society. We are a valuable part of the nation's (and the world's) mental capital. I'm very grateful for having had the opportunity to participate, and am thoroughly convinced of the benefits of engaging older people in research into the ageing process. In retrospect it would seem perverse to do otherwise!

The student registers the personal benefit of being involved in terms of his own knowledge and insight not just into the Open Learning Programme itself but also into the broader issues of ageing. The enthusiasm for how participation in education can enhance wellbeing among older people is movingly articulated. The student has become 'an ambassador for the whole process', an agent of change among his own circles of friends. Perhaps most power-fully, through his very deep participation as interviewee, as reader and as data analyst he is now much more aware of the importance of challenging nega-tive stereotypes of older people and of older people themselves being actively involved in doing this through being directly involved in the research.

Another participant suggested that we 'use the primary source of the stu-dents to build up a picture of growing old, their experience of retirement, illness, and thoughts of mortality'. During the special courses, students were asked to comment on their own experience in comparison to what writers and artists were saying, but this could, perhaps, have been more thoroughgo-ing. It must also be reiterated that many older people interviewed were not all that happy about being defined as older people, and among those who did address the specific issues of ageing, the responses were mostly positive.

One student set a clear and logical agenda for further research:

> I wish that this sort of project could be extended into the less affluent areas of our community. Outreach would be the next progression. I would love to see those who have perhaps missed out on a formal edu-cation being able to participate later in life as a second chance option.

Conclusions

The responses from participants about being involved in this co-research project were overwhelmingly positive. Participants repeatedly expressed their appreciation of being able to voice their own views and also to hear the perspectives, sometimes quite contrasting, coming from other students. Many participants also registered their appreciation at being asked to become involved in a research project that allowed them not only to reflect on their personal experience and wisdom but also to be part of a piece of work that was useful, that had potential benefits for other older people and for society. Most viewed the project as both interesting and worthwhile. The majority felt they were able to draw on existing skills, while for others, the project created the opportunity to learn new skills. And this realisation undoubtedly enhanced their wellbeing and sense of self-esteem and confidence.

Beneath the responses it also became evident that the more extensive the volunteer's involvement, the more positive and extensive was their reflection as participants. The greater the time, effort and involvement, the more posi-tive the response; but that in no way vitiates the response of all the partici-pants. It is vital in co-research projects that we empower learners to choose the kind of engagement they want and the extent of it.

One aspect for future reference might be that greater emphasis on train-ing would be appreciated and might lead to an even more positive expe-rience, though this must also be balanced with the scale of the research project and the commitment asked of volunteer co-researchers. We can see our co-researchers in action in Figures 5.1, 5.2, and 5.3.

Figure 5.1 Recording the learning.

Figure 5.2 Pass me the jam: peer tutors Dr Michael Scott and Dr Cecilia Ward take the floor at one of the special courses on ageing.

Figure 5.3 The four musketeers: Asma Niazi, Allen Young, Pauline Prior and Tess Maginess, having a small break in the editing.

References

Bindels, J., Baur, V., Cox, K., Heijing, S. and Abma, T. (2014) 'Older people as co-researchers: A collaborative journey', *Ageing and Society*, 34 (6), pp. 951–973.

Bishop, D., Crawford, K., Jenner, N., Liddle, N., Russell, E. and Woollard, M. (Undated) *Engaging students in quality processes*, York: Higher Education Academy [online]. Available at http://jisctechdis.ac.uk/assets/Documents/disciplines/social-sciences/ELiSS0403Practice_paper02.pdf (Accessed: 14 July 2015).

Blair, T. and Minkler, M. (2009) 'Participatory action research with older adults: Key principles in practice', *The Gerontologist*, 49 (5), pp. 651–662.

Boulton-Lewis, G. and Tam, M. (eds.) (2012) *Active ageing, active learning: Issues and challenges* (Education in the Asia-Pacific Region: Issues, Concerns and Prospects), New York: Springer.

Eliot, T.S. (1918) 'The Hawthorne aspect', *The Little Review*, 5 (4), p. 49.

Ellis, C., Adams, T. and Bochner, P. (2011) 'Autoethnography: An overview', *Forum: Qualitative Social Research* 12 (1), Art. 1, unpaged. Available at http://www.qualitative-research.net/index.php/fqs/article/view/1589/3095 (Accessed: 29 March 2016).

Fielding, M. (2001) 'Students as radical agents of change', *Journal of Educational Change*, 2, pp. 123–141.

Gapp, R. and Fisher, R. (2006) 'Achieving excellence through innovative approaches to student involvement in course evaluation within the tertiary education sector', *Quality Assurance in Education*, 14 (2), pp. 156–166.

Gutman, G. (2014) 'Involving older adults as co-researchers in social work education', *Educational Gerontology*, 40 (3), pp. 186–197.

Healey, M., Flint, A. and Harrington, K. (2014) *Engagement through partnership: Students as partners in learning and teaching in higher education*, York: Higher Education Academy.

Jarvis, J., Dickerson, C. and Stockwell, L. (2013) 'Staff-student partnership in practice in higher education: The impact on learning and teaching', *Procedia – Social and Behavioural Sciences*, 90, pp. 220–225.

Kallas, E. (2011) 'The power of student participation', *Connect [Victorian Student Representative Council]*, 89, pp. 19–20.

Kennedy, J.F. (1961) 'Inaugural address' [online]. Available at http://www.bartleby.com/124/pres56.html (Accessed: 3 December 2015).

Littlechild, R., Tanner, D. and Hall, K. (2015) 'Co-research with older people: Perspectives on impact', *Qualitative Social Work*, 14 (1), pp. 18–35.

Maginess, T. (2006) 'Are ye mad? A meta-analysis of an emancipatory research project undertaken by service users and "voluntary" carers', in *Intercultural perspectives on research into adult learning: A global dialogue*, SCUTREA 2006 Annual Conference Proceedings, Leeds: University of Leeds, pp. 263–270.

Maginess, T. (2010) 'Medium as message: Making an "emancipating" film on mental health and distress', *Educational Action Research*, 18 (4), pp. 497–515.

Maunder, R. (2015) 'Working with students as partners in pedagogic research: Staff and student experiences of participating in an institutional bursary scheme', *Journal of Educational Innovation, Partnership and Change*, 1 (1), pp. 1–7.

Maunder, R., Cunliffe, M., Galvin, J., Mjali, S. and Rogers, J. (2013) 'Listening to student voices: Student researchers exploring undergraduate experiences of university transition', *Higher Education*, 66, pp. 139–152.

McClusky, H.Y. (1971) 'The adult as learner', in Seashore, S.E. and McNeill, R.J. (eds.) *Management of the urban crisis*, New York: The Free Press, pp. 27–39.

Messiou, K. (2013) 'Working with students as co-researchers in schools: A matter of inclusion', *International Journal of Inclusive Education*, 18 (6), pp. 601–613.

Taylor, P. and Wilding, D. (2009) *Rethinking the values of higher education: The student as collaborator and producer? Undergraduate research as a case study*, Gloucester: The Quality Assurance Agency for Higher Education.

Trowler, V. and Trowler, P. (2010) *Student engagement literature review*, York: HEA. Available at https://www.heacademy.ac.uk/sites/default/files/StudentEngagement LiteratureReview_1.pdf (Accessed: 4 June 2014).

Walker, A. (2007) 'Editorial', *Age and Ageing [British Geriatrics Society]*, 36, pp. 481–483.

Chapter 6

Conclusions and recommendations

The first part of this chapter provides some of the answers to the question asked in this research project – does participation in the Open Learning Programme at Queen's University Belfast contribute to the wellbeing and wisdom of older learners? The second part of the chapter extrapolates from this one example to the wider issues facing providers of courses for older learners, with a view to increasing participation in courses which offer life-enhancing experiences for older learners. The final discussion is on the process of co-research – what it meant in this project and what it could mean for future work with older learners.

The overall conclusion of the research is that learners overwhelmingly attest that participation in the programme contributes to both wellbeing and wisdom. This confirms what the experts say, but does in very specific ways. Just providing learning programmes or 'opportunities' does not, in itself, improve the wellbeing and wisdom of older learners; a whole range of factors need to be present for wellbeing and wisdom to be genuinely enhanced.

Crucial to an understanding of these factors are not just the views of older learners but also their active participation as co-researchers in the whole process of defining and articulating what factors are important for them, not just for programme providers, whether formal or informal. Arguably, less formal programmes may be better at keeping at the centre the views of older learners, but we hope we have demonstrated that a more formal programme, based in a university, has the capacity to be shaped by older learners and to respond to what they value from their experience and knowledge. Older learners, involved in every aspect of the research process, have demonstrated that they know how not only to critique their entire learning situation and extrapolate a rich set of conclusions, but also, vitally, to engage in the complex business of becoming co-researchers. They have, thus, shown the way in terms of genuine empowerment and have demonstrated their dynamic potential to open a whole new front in the resistance to negative stereotypes, in the paradigm shift from 'otherness' to inclusion. As has been stated many times in this book, there is still very little in the literature about older learners as co-researchers. There are few examples of this new domain. This is a new front; their innovation could be an innovation for everyone. That brings wisdom and joy to us all.

From the data, it is evident that the Open Learning Programme represented for many learners both an 'age-appropriate' set of learning opportunities and approaches *and* a resistance to the negative stereotype that older people cannot learn, or don't want to learn. It is the capacity for learning, the will to learn that, it seems, constitutes their definition of staying young and, consequently, their sense of wellbeing. But this is a complex nexus; the older learners are fully aware that they are older; courses on ageing may reinforce internalised negative representations of older people, notwithstanding the fact that such courses and the literature in educational gerontology challenge the negative 'hegemony'. This ambivalence has not been evident in the literature from educational gerontology, though, as we saw earlier, it is poignantly articulated in the work of writers like Segal (2013).

Learners also tell us that they want courses which are age-appropriate, and this seems to mean, on the other side of the coin, that they want to keep young in their mind and in their spirit: embracing new ideas, skills and knowledge, keeping up to date, having their own views challenged and contradicted. This study, *because* it is conducted by older learners, has revealed the paradox, one that all working with older people need to be more keenly and sensitively aware of.

What emerge as important to the learners' wellbeing are opportunities to pursue their own individual learning pathway, to finally learn the things they always wanted to learn or to deepen and widen their appreciation of a subject dear to them all through their lives. And for learners the engagement in a process of lifelong or continuing learning is crucial too. That process is for some learners a golden thread connecting them with a lifetime passion, professional or personal; for others, the excitement derives from returning to fields they once loved, and for others in discovering new subjects. For many learners it would seem to be also the simple and complex belief that wellbeing is grounded in a profound sense that, to be human, we all need to keep learning.

But the 'how' as well as the 'what' of learning is clearly also critical. The learners value participating in a programme which offers a variety of teaching and learning styles, but which values their long-won expertise and knowledge and allows them to interact and co-construct learning, as reported by Trowler and Trowler (2010). Teaching and learning styles which took account of older learners' specific needs and aspirations were also highlighted. And the 'how' is also very much about the opportunities for social interaction – in the class and beyond the class. While not all learners thought that this was a key factor in wellbeing, many did. And, significantly, the combination of the educational and social dimensions was what older learners valued – just as younger learners might. The learning environment – support systems, best practice responsiveness towards students with disabilities, welcoming and helpful support staff, a culture of listening and responding to issues raised by students, comfortable rooms, access to catering facilities – was a salient but important factor in wellbeing.

Our learners reflected on the complex obstacles which might discourage participation among those who do not engage with this or other programmes; a perception of universities as remote and 'not for us', financial constraints, caring responsibilities, and health problems and some very interesting suggestions were advanced about how we might encourage more older people to engage with lifelong learning as a way of enhancing their wellbeing.

Arguing the case for the impact of participation on wellbeing

There is no doubt that many of the responses from learners convey a sense that the Open Learning Programme enhances their wellbeing – their sense of enjoyment and their sense of rising to a challenge. But some learners explicitly pointed to the wellbeing and mental health advantages. Here is what some of them said:

> There are loads of mental health benefits, mood improvements. The positive health benefits of having some purposeful activity and something interesting to work on is well researched.

> [E]ntertaining and educational, improves esteem and self-worth, does wonders for you. You are part of the world, helps brain to work well, love of learning re-kindled, so full of life, so exciting.

> Life-enhancing.

> The aesthetic and emotional value is very high, expanding one's creative and experiential world – doing what enhances your mental health, social wellbeing and spiritual wellbeing.

> [The programme] maintains your health and longevity, learning is keeping the brain active, one of the three pillars of good retirement, life should be a learning process, the evidence suggests learning is a lifelong process and good for wellbeing.

One student felt that the programme was extremely important for empowerment and for the link it provides to the community. He went on to say that there was a real challenge to education in relation to the older generation and that the position of Open Learning needs to be better recognised and 'elevated' within the university. It may be noted that the interviewee, who has given permission to waive his anonymity, was a former vice-chancellor of Queen's University, Professor Sir George Bain. He added that if he were vice-chancellor again, he would give Open Learning more prominence.

Again, focusing on the age-related dimension, one learner said that studying literature 'was lovely, a pleasure for the Third Age years'.

It is hard not to notice, in this last set of comments, how the register of the prose has risen, reflecting the excitement and joy the learners want to convey to other older people, and their conviction that participating in this kind of lifelong learning programme offers undoubted wellbeing and health benefits. It would be tempting to extrapolate that learners are telling us that there is a kind of virtuous equation through which a combination of keeping the mind active through learning plus social contact equals maintenance of health and longevity. So what have the experts said?

Field (2012, pp. 11–12) points to the growing body of evidence suggesting improvements to wellbeing from participation in learning. Boulton-Lewis (2012, pp. 21–22) refers to a number of studies, including Butler (2002), which confirms that engagement in meaningful activities contributes to good health, satisfaction with life and longevity, and reducing the costs of physical and emotional illness. She refers also to the World Health Organization (2002), which proposed that active ageing was based on optimising opportunities for health, participation and security. Boulton-Lewis (2012) also draws on evidence from Australia, America and the UK, including the work of Rowe and Kahn (1997) for the MacArthur Research Network on an Aging Society. Self-reliance and self-confidence are also boosted. She concludes that although the evidence that lifelong learning has a positive impact on cognitive powers is largely co-relational, it should assist in many positive ways, including inter alia: self-confidence, coping strategies, maintaining cognitive function and knowledge, and health management. The British Psychological Society (BeLL Project, 2014) reported on the benefits of the Benefits of Lifelong Learning (BeLL) Project, carried out in Finland. According to the report, researchers at the University of Eastern Finland collected data from three universities, three research institutes and five adult education organisations as part of the BeLL project, resulting in 8,646 valid questionnaires and 82 interviews across ten countries.

The researchers examined the responses of adult learners participating in non-vocational courses over a year and discovered that studying boosted their self-confidence and wellbeing, as well as expanding their social networks. Tolerance for others grew, learners paid more attention to their health and some even reported changes in their work and career opportunities. Adult education was found to be particularly beneficial for people with a lower educational level. The age of the participants also influenced the benefits they achieved – younger people said it made them feel more in control of their lives, while older age groups reported adult education as being able to soften the transitions related to ageing, such as bereavement. The report argues that liberal adult education should be better taken into consideration in both national and EU-level education policy, and that a more systematic approach should be taken towards utilising its clear benefits on wellbeing.

Steptoe, Deaton and Stone (2015) argue for the link between wellbeing, good health and longevity. Findsen (2005, p. 19) also makes the case for the benefits of education with older people in terms of better health and wellbeing and the potential cost benefits in terms of savings on medical care.

Field (2009, p. 11) points to the 'growing body of evidence on the relationship between learning and well-being', as well as on the impact of learning on factors that help to promote wellbeing. Social interaction, self-esteem and feelings of competency are cited as important outcomes. Overall, his paper argues that 'wellbeing' is increasingly being recognised as an important target for interventions of all kinds, and that adult learning is a significant tool for enhancing it.

The European EuBIA project also reported the positive effects of older people engaging in learning (Benyson *et al.*, 2010). And according to Staehelin (2005, p. 175), 'the positive effects of educational programmes for the older population will substantially contribute to health and wellbeing in late life. Probably the most important benefit is that elderly citizens will find it easier to find meaning in their life.' Withnal (2004) argues for the education of older people as a form of empowerment, especially in terms of its role in counteracting marginalisation, dependency and poverty. She argues for educational gerontology as a means to raise consciousness, help older people achieve positive roles and enhance quality of life and self-fulfilment. A study of Singapore retirees attending the Young at Heart college also reported enhances self-confidence, a growing wisdom and capacity from being involved in learning and an ability to use the learning within society (Lee, Wei and Hu, 2014). Aldridge and Hughes (2012, p. 2) comment that the benefits of engaging in education are not just confined to those who engage in courses: 'We know that many of those who get involved in learning will have a positive impact on others around them.'

The wellbeing benefits of getting involved in education are now, increasingly, being recognised in the media, though we have a fair distance to travel in terms of counteracting the negative stereotypes. Wellbeing may even prolong your life. Von Radowitz (2014, p. 19) reports on research published in *The Lancet* by Steptoe *et al.* (2015) that 'eudemonic' wellbeing – having a purpose in life, doing something you think is worthwhile – is much more likely to contribute to longevity. Charities like the Future Foundation (2014, p. 15) also advocate the benefits of education for older people, especially in terms of social contact.

Communicating the joy of learning?

Many learners said that they talked about the Open Learning Programme to other people. For some, this had to do with how they extended their learning and maybe relived the excitement of their reading and the class itself, through discussing the topic with friends and learning. So, for example, one learner said, 'Yes, incessantly, we are lucky to have this on the doorstep,' while another said that he enjoyed talking about the courses to his wife, who comes with him to the courses. We have all heard the expression 'she lives and breathes' literature or gardening or metaphysics or sport, and it is to me truly delightful that learners continue to gain pleasure and further understanding from 'revisiting' what they are learning with friends or family. It may be a very simple point, but is it not the case, at a basic human level, that our wellbeing increases when we are doing something we enjoy, including talking about why we enjoy it?

Students as ambassadors?

Some respondents interpreted the question about whether they talk to friends or family about their learning as having to do with encouraging others to participate in the programme. To put this another way, they 'heard' the question as being primarily to do with promoting the programme. Among these responses, some learners were quite qualified in their answers, suggesting that they would talk to others, but only if they thought they would be interested in the courses. Two learners said that they did talk to others, but this fell on deaf ears, while another said that his friends were engineers and were not interested in books (i.e. literature). However, other students said that they did try to encourage people to enrol. A few students noted that they had either been successfully 'recruited' by family or friends or had persuaded other people to come along. With regard to the more positive, if qualified responses, we might wish to consider the question of whether learners should, in fact, be ambassadors for the programme, and if so, what might be the best ways of doing this?

I am of the view that learners should most certainly not feel any pressure about acting as ambassadors, never mind recruiting sergeants. However, we know from the data that quite a few learners said that they themselves had first heard about the programme through 'word of mouth' from family or friends. And it may be for our students that their circle of friends and family are not interested in the same subjects as the learners and so the programme holds no attraction, despite the enthusiasm of the learner in talking about Yeats or the representation of dementia in *King Lear*. And, on the other side, it is clear from the data that there are many learners who have, so to speak, crossed the 'floor of the house', having had a career as an engineer or a doctor or a dentists' receptionist or a geography teacher or as a nurse or a hairdresser, but who always wanted to study literature or history or to learn how to play the guitar.

I wonder if this very commendable subject-driven agenda can have the effect of narrowing the focus a little too much at times. So, learners tend to go straight to those sections of the brochure which list the courses in the subject areas which interest them and so are not always completely aware that this programme, like many other adult education and adult learning programmes, offers a very wide range of subjects and topics, some of which may appeal to friends and family. It is not, I repeat, the responsibility of our students to read the whole brochure and then go among their friends and family, proclaiming apostolically that there is something in there for everyone. Rather, this points back to the 'providers' of the programme in terms of how we can do a bit better in making students aware of not just what they have kindly praised, the depth through which particular subjects are approached, but also the *range* of subjects and topics and learning pathways available to them as well as to their friends and family.

Recommendations

The first set of recommendations will relate to how the Open Learning Programme at Queen's University, as an example of formal education for older learners, could be improved to further enhance the wellbeing and wisdom of older learners. One set of recommendations will be addressed primarily to providers of such programmes. We will then offer some recommendations to other stakeholders, including policymakers and funders, before addressing some recommendations to older people themselves. Withnal and Percy (1994), drawing on Harrison (1988), Glendenning and Battersby (1990), Percy (1990), Schuller and Bostyn (1992) and Batersby (1993), have called for the formulation of governmental policy statements which would encourage greater expansion of older people's educational activity. Citing McGivney (1990) and Schuller and Bostyn (1992), they also urge educational institutions to be more welcoming, accessible, aware, encouraging, supportive, responsive, willing to take risks and flexible. They also highlight the importance of harnessing the skills, knowledge and experience of older people in order to improve provision.

Recommendations to providers of learning opportunities to and with older people

We may note that the United Nations Madrid Plan (United Nations, 2002, unpaged) exhorts educators to recognise and include in their courses the contributions made by persons of all ages, including older persons. Here, then, are our recommendations:

- *Create choice for older students: individual learning pathways.*

   Providers, whether universities or informal study groups, need to offer as wide-ranging a curriculum or choice of subjects as possible; providers, whether universities, or informal study groups need to constantly review the choice of subjects offered, if learning is truly to be shaped by the learners and learners are to be enabled to direct their own learning and engage in a continuous journey of lifelong learning. However, it must also be recognised that too large a choice can result in larger numbers of classes being cancelled and that tutors may not always be available locally. Those compiling the prospectus should highlight, through cross-referencing, subjects which are allied, but described in a different section or under a different heading in the course listings and descriptions. It must also be recognised that not all institutions and organisations have the finance and resources to expand the choice of subjects. We will address this in the recommendations to funders and policymakers.

• *Provide learning programmes that are structured and sustainable.*

Endeavour to create continuity and sustainability through regular and ongoing programmes: this is to enable learners to experience the value of a structured, sustainable framework for learning. One-off programmes or initiatives, however enjoyable and important, do not offer the necessary continuity to enable learners to either develop a learning pathway or engage in a genuine process of lifelong learning. That older people want to engage in learning over a long period is amply demonstrated in the testimony of the learners and, indeed, in the high quotient of 'return learners' we have in the Open Learning Programme. This is not a facet that has been much studied, and it is to be hoped that this piece of research will reinforce for providers and policymakers the crucial importance of recognising that if real wellbeing is to be achieved and wisdom is to be harvested, investment in education for older people is a long-term process, just as older people's learning is, in their view, a long-term process. Providers, therefore, need to maintain a commitment to older learners. Queen's University, Belfast, has honoured that commitment since its inception. We will address this also in the recommendations to funders and policymakers.

• *Ensure that programmes are characterised by high standards of teaching.*

Regularly review standards of teaching to ensure that learners get access to high-quality teaching. Mechanisms should include careful selection of tutors and courses which respond to suggestions from learners, proper induction and training of tutors, mentoring of tutors, student evaluations, listening and responding to any issues and problems as soon as they arise, communication with tutors about what works well and what does not and regular moderation, both internal and external. Providers should also review their programme offering to ensure a good balance between practical and more intellectual subjects and introduce topical themes – for example, we ran a suite of special courses in 2014 to commemorate the outbreak of the First World War; these spanned history, literature and the visual arts. Providers should also ensure that the programme is kept fresh by introducing new tutors and subjects, perhaps enabling new tutors to teach one or two classes within an established programme before taking on their own course. With panel-taught courses, providers need to search for the very best talent. For instance, in the World Literature course and in the Blackbird Bookclub, we have high-calibre guest writers and broadcasters.

- *Offer a variety of teaching and learning styles, especially participative or active learning.*

  Provide learners with a variety of teaching styles, bearing in mind the particular constraints and potential of both large classes and smaller group teaching and learning. Older learners favour transmissive approaches when they are communicated in dynamic and entertaining styles, because the charismatic teacher, the teacher with the 'x factor', can remind them of their more delightful experiences of education. Transmissive and constructionist approaches can be blended and offer learners opportunities for active and participative learning so that students attain new knowledge and information, have a guide or pilot for their learning, but also have the sense that their experience, knowledge and skills are valued and are incorporated into the learning process. In this way students can learn from one another, and the teacher is a facilitator, empowering the learners to discover what they between them know and how they can correct the teacher and enable the teacher to learn.

- *Empower learners to co-construct the curriculum.*

  Offer learners opportunities to contribute to or co-construct the curriculum so that they can extend their sense of ownership and control and thus feel more valued. This will result in a far more equal set of relationships between teacher and student and also enrich the range and depth of the learning co-constructed between teacher and student. To be sure, this plunges the teacher into a *terra incognita*; construct a lecture about a novel or a poem or a play which they do not know or know and do not like. But surely this places the teacher in exactly the same position as the learner, confronted with a curriculum that is, at best, a bit of a challenge. Well, if we are any good as teachers, we must also be learners, prepared to confront what we do not know. And, I might add, this is but a tiny part of the challenge of growing older. But if we play the game of facing the unknown, the feared, with a ludic spirit, with a sense of what might be gained rather than lost, the odds are we will not come away with our minds and hearts and spirits demeaned.

- *Encourage peer teaching and learning.*

  The University of the Third Age (U3A), the Osher learning communities and the Young at Heart College in Singapore have set a great example.

Formal learning programmes should learn from this more participative approach, though careful planning, training and mentoring are needed to ensure that standards are high. Older people deserve the very best and have demonstrated that they too can learn, can refine their experience and knowledge to become peer tutors and researchers. Providers need to do much more to encourage a blending of the virtues of non-formal learning programmes with more formal university-based provision. An accredited programme in teaching and learning with older people might be one way of addressing this, but older people need to be able to access this programme free of charge. Better linkages between formal and non-formal providers also need to be promoted, perhaps drawing together adult education experts in organisations like NIACE (National Institute of Adult and Continuing Education) and the whole range of formal and informal providers with older people's organisations and centres for ageing, internationally.

- *Share the passion and joy of learning.*

Providers need to value and share the learners' enthusiasm and joy in learning new, ideas, skills and knowledge, in broadening their horizons and in being challenged by different points of view and new insights. Providers need to encourage tutors to be enthusiastic and passionate about their subject. Tutors need to be made more aware of the literature on andragogy and geragogy and how this might inflect and improve their practice. There is still too great a gap between theory and practice. At the same time, care and sensitivity are needed to take account of the ambivalence among older learners themselves about being 'labelled' as older people. And providers also need to encourage learners to develop confidence in realising that they are able to learn and how this can challenge stereotypes of older people as decrepit or incapable of learning.

- *Assess assessment.*

Providers need to consider methods of assessment carefully; learners welcome the freedom from examinations and the joy of learning for its own sake. However, some students also enjoy opportunities to crystallise and reflect on their learning – for example, through writing essays. Imaginative forms of assessment should also be considered – for example, reflective journals or hands-on projects, such as film-making or music-making projects. If learners feel more comfortable with visual or aural assignments, they should be offered the choice. So, for example, creating a storyboard about a novel they have read or writing a song based on a character in history may be just as effective as a straightforward essay. In practical or applied subjects, such as first aid or digital photography, assessments need to depart from traditional academic 'essay' based modes and embrace a more empirical calculus. Assessment should not be a chore but a way through which learners can clarify and articulate what they have learned in an enjoyable way.

- *Provide backup materials, such as notes or handouts.*

  In reflecting on how learning can be as student-centred as possible for older people, providers should incorporate features which could make learning easier and more enjoyable for older people. This could include introducing PowerPoints and multimedia materials so that learners can access the topic through a variety of modes. The provision of backup materials, such as notes and handouts, is also vital in assisting learners to retain and reflect on the topics covered. Since not all learners have access to computers, materials should be provided in both online and hard-copy formats, with the additional choice of large print or audio versions for those who may find alternative formats more accessible and enjoyable.

- *Offer flexible timetabling.*

  Older people, as we have said before, are not all the same; some prefer to attend classes during the day, while evenings or weekends suit others better. Providers need to take the wishes of their learners into account and offer flexible timetabling so that older people can pursue other activities or avoid having to attend night classes in winter, when they may be more susceptible to feeling the cold or worrying about their safety. A mix of short weekend courses and more lengthy 10-, 20- and 40-hour programmes spread over several weeks also creates more choice for students. Short taster-type courses are also a great way to 'test the market' for new courses. Courses on environment and practical visual arts courses are best suited for autumn and spring, when the weather is, at least theoretically, milder. Opportunities for learners to get out and about are often popular, and field trip–type courses are a great way to enhance physical wellbeing too. It is recognised that not all providers are in a position to offer a huge range, and we will address this in the next set of recommendations.

- *Pitch the level of learning to allow for a range of knowledge and skills.*

  Pitching learning at the right level is a very difficult skill, but providers need to recognise the range of experience, knowledge and skill within any one group of students. Frequently checking if ideas or skills have been understood is one important way for teachers to gauge the pitch and to adjust the pace or style of the teaching. Peer learning can assist in this by encouraging students to discuss ideas between them. Small group work can also enable students to assist each other with skills-based tasks.

- *Create a range of 'levels' for subjects.*

  Providers should, if at all possible, offer opportunities for learners to 'enter' a subject at different levels, thus recognising that some may already have previous knowledge or skill in a particular area and enabling students to progress from one level to the next. This is especially important in language teaching, where learners may not actually know, initially, what level they are at. Students should be permitted, as they are in the Open Learning Programme, to sample different levels for a week or two before deciding what suits them best and be enabled to transfer from one level to another.

- *Consider whether special courses focused on ageing will appeal to learners.*

  As can be seen from our data, the jury is out, but some providers may well be working with groups of learners who would find such courses beneficial. The important thing is to consult with learners and pilot such courses. As we have seen, some of the literature suggests that older people benefit from courses specifically focused on issues to do with ageing. But our data offers a less conclusive picture. Indeed, for some, special courses on ageing constitute a chill factor. Our learners reflect an ambivalence doubtless characteristic of older people generally. So we must engage with older people themselves and tailor courses to what they want or need. Some may, indeed, want or need practical courses about a whole range of issues which are age-related. Our courses on pensions are always popular, but some, as our data suggests, may have figured out how to handle retirement and active ageing and just want to study what they fancy. And some see the very process of engaging with learning as a way of challenging ageism. Providers, therefore, need to think both within the box and 'beyond the box' here and listen to what older people say about what they actually enjoy as well as what others, who do not have the experience of being older, think is best for them.

- *Ensure that there is good access and support for students with disabilities.*

  Providers need to make sure that there are dedicated, professional support services for learners with disabilities in place. Again, this proceeds from a learner-centred ethos; learners' needs and aspirations need to be identified and addressed on an individual basis and before they enrol so that their particular support needs can be met. Buildings also need to be accessible for students with disabilities. Again there are funding implications, which we will address ahead.

- *Provide a welcoming atmosphere.*

  This means training and developing a culture among support staff or 'front-of-house' staff or volunteers in which the learner is seen as a valued supporter of the learning programme. Taking time with older students and being friendly, empathic and courteous with them are crucial. Responding to any issues raised by learners as quickly and effectively as possible is also vital so that learners feel that they are being listened to and that their views are important.

- *Ensure that teaching and learning rooms are warm and comfortable and as conveniently located as possible.*

Few providers have complete freedom or funding to offer 'dream classrooms'. However, older people do sometimes feel the cold more than younger students and factors like seating can also be an issue – two hours on a hard plastic chair is not ideal. Providers need to try to ensure that classrooms are as far away from the less pleasant contemporary waiting room and the old hard bench of unhappy early memory.

Providers need to locate the courses as conveniently as possible for older learners to get to them. This may mean in some cases that a central location is preferable, but there may be other considerations, such as parking or a 'chill factor' associated with certain locations or settings. Providers should also consider offering, if possible, some education-in-the-community or outreach courses to create better access, especially for those considering engaging with education for the first time, who might find a university or other institutional setting intimidating, as well as for those in rural areas or in areas that are disadvantaged. There may be resource issues here; collaborations and partnership working with other organisations in the local area can often create potential for enlarging the stock of comfortable and convenient venues. It is recognised, however, that funding can be an issue and we will address this in the next section.

- *Provide facilities for tea and coffee.*

As we have seen, the social dimension of older people's learning is very important and getting together for tea or coffee or a bite of lunch is a great way to encourage social interaction. Older people are sometimes also more in need of a warm drink and are not so used to the long fasts that young people seem to be able to endure. Facilities should be provided as near as possible to all teaching and learning rooms, though it is recognised that in a large, spread-out campus, this is not always feasible, especially at night. There may be funding implications for some providers and we will address these ahead.

- *Provide additional opportunities for learners to interact socially.*

This may be in the form of informal get-togethers, end-of-year parties, class outings and field trips. Better co-operation with organisations like the Elderhostel movement could achieve some good outcomes. Better links with older people's organisations, locally, nationally and internationally, could also yield new connections and co-operation. It is recognised, however, that funding and staff resources may be issues here, so see ahead under Recommendations to Policymakers.

- *Provide good access to information about courses.*

Providers need to put themselves in the position of the learner. Information should be easily available. While older learners enjoy mixing with younger generations, providers should also target information about courses and programmes to places and facilities used by older people, including health centres, cafes, hotels and pubs, church groups, older people's organisations and social and community centres and libraries. The format also needs to be accessible to ensure that older people can access information in whatever way is most natural and convenient for them: print, audio and online. Alternative formats for people with disabilities also need to be offered. Brochures and promotional materials need to do more to emphasise that the programmes are genuinely open, not just to the 'usual suspects' but to the whole community. Again there are potential funding implications, which we will address in the next section.

- *Offer flexible ways to enrol.*

This means offering a range of options to potential learners: enrolling in person, by telephone, in writing and online. As we have seen, not all older people 'do' computers. Many do not and should not be dragooned into doing so or made to feel excluded. Providers need to recognise that it is their responsibility to communicate with the 'market' of older learners, and to do so on their terms. From the perspective of social responsibility and outreach, providers need to give respect to all who are willing to engage, at their own expense, in learning.

- *Provide taster courses to groups not currently engaged in education and learning.*

Taster courses may be one way of encouraging those not currently involved in lifelong learning to get involved. This seems a 'no-brainer', but the reality is that most learning organisations simply do not have the staff and financial resources to deliver such courses. It is recognised that there are funding implications for some providers and these will be addressed in the next sections.

- *Offer affordable courses.*

While some providers do not charge, many do. Cost may well be an issue for some older people not currently engaged in learning. As we have seen earlier, cost needs to be considered in terms of not just the price of the course but also transport, respite and accessible transport. The lives of older people are, more often than not, complicated by caring responsibilities, compromised health, loss, loneliness and a sense of worthlessness.

- *Tackle attitudinal barriers for those not currently participating in education.*

Providers need to do more to disseminate the message in publicity that courses are not just for certain 'privileged' sections of older people but that people from all backgrounds are very welcome (Findsen *et al.*, 2011). As one strategy for breaking down barriers, providers may wish to consider developing 'student ambassador' schemes along the lines of the 'older people's champions' schemes operating in some further education colleges, as noted in the Northern Ireland Assembly's Active Ageing Strategy (Office of the First Minister, 2014). This may not be possible in every setting, but the value of peer persuasion can be very powerful. There are potential resource issues here, so see ahead in the next set of recommendations to policymakers.

Recommendations to policymakers and education funders

- *Engage in a culture shift.*

Funders and policymakers need to do more to appreciate the positive benefits to society of engaging older people in sustainable and enjoyable learning. They need to view active participation in learning as one of a number of measures which could holistically improve the position of older people, enhance their wellbeing and wisdom and enable them to contribute more actively to society. The UK Department of Health (2013) published a response to the report *Ready for Ageing*, but it is notable that there is nothing in this response which mentions education or lifelong learning. Other commentators point to the current governmental focus on vocational and employment skills for older people (Nolan, 2007; Nash, 2015). While this is important, as argued by Hyde and Phillipson (2014), there needs also to be a focus on non-vocational learning and education with older people. The total amount spent on education for people over 30 is a very small portion of governmental education and skills budgets (NICVA, 2015, p. 21). There do appear to be some government-funded programmes operating in Northern Ireland – for example, activity classes for older people run by local authorities – and it could be argued that the block grant to universities does support lifelong learning.

According to Tuckett (2014) adult learners as far back as 1992 were suggesting that their learning should be self-directed, that they could be the best judges of what was worth studying. Tuckett argued that learners and potential learners have a right to claim a modest investment from government so that they could follow their own learning pathway. There have been, over the years, criticisms of the lack of governmental focus on lifelong learning. Nash (2015) cites Scott (2015), who expresses disappointment about lifelong learning provision for older people, and Nash, echoing Schuller and Watson (2009), calls for a re-balancing to create more opportunities for older people to access education and learning.

There have been some promising projects funded in the UK targeting older people, including the New Dynamics of Ageing project and the Joseph Rowntree–funded project on older people as researchers (Leamy and Clough, 2006). Davies (2014, p. 4) draws attention to the European Union's many strategies and policies about active ageing, which include lifelong learning and training opportunities for older people. The EU has also funded some initiatives, specifically targeting older people and lifelong learning, including the Lifelong Learning Programme, which ran 2007–2013 and which, it is claimed, will continue under the Erasmus programme (European Commission, undated), and, more specifically in the area of working with older people as researchers, the EuBIA project discussed earlier (Benyson *et al.*, 2010). The Madrid Plan (United Nations, 2002, unpaged) calls for the experience, skills and wisdom of older people to be respected in terms of their contribution to society as a whole (Article 10). It calls also for access to education and training opportunities, with sustainable social support to be provided (Article 12), and it asks for the educational system to respond to changing demographics. A more coordinated strategy, embedded also at local, regional and national government levels is, however, needed, dedicated to learning and education for and with older people.

- *Address the low rates of participation in learning by older people.*

Considering the low rates of participation, especially by older people from less privileged backgrounds, we would recommend that governments address this major issue at a strategic level through the following specific measures:

- *Ring-fence resources.*

Governments need to develop a dedicated mechanism or ring-fenced fund to provide realistic and adequate funding to enable greater numbers of older people to participate in learning, perhaps an extension of Schuller and Watson's advocacy of 'learning entitlements' (2009), though not restricted to vocational or employment-related learning, but rather framed by an understanding that we need to invest in older people if they are to genuinely play their part in society. This funding needs to take into account how costs for courses could be subvented, but also how support costs, such as respite for those with caring responsibilities, assistance with travel costs and assistance with venue and extra tutor costs, could enable the development of outreach or education-in-the-community courses. Crucial to the success of any new fund is that it be administered in a non-bureaucratic way, perhaps related to schemes like direct payments.

- *Work in partnership with older people.*

  Listening to older people is crucial. Governments also need to engage in a coordinated approach so that all organisations and experts in the field of older people's learning are actively engaged (Findsen, 2014). Governments need to convene a standing group or other such multi-agency grouping involving a range of education and learning providers, older people's groups, centres for ageing and educational gerontology and charities across the UK and with partners internationally with a view to developing a coherent multi-agency strategy for involving greater numbers of older people in learning, especially the most disadvantaged.

- *Provide grants to universities and other providers to enable them to enhance their provision.* This would include funding to:

    (i) improve facilities to enable better access for older learners
    (ii) enable providers to employ extra tutors
    (iii) offer outreach or education-in-the-community courses, including taster courses
    (iv) enable providers to employ development workers, older people's champions and student ambassadors
    (v) contribute to overhead costs to ensure sustainability in terms of provision and support for learners
    (vi) provide dedicated, professional support services for learners with disabilities
    (vii) provide extra facilities such as tea and coffee and for 'value-added' social interaction through field trips and study visits
    (viii) generate better publicity about lifelong learning courses
    (ix) create schemes for student ambassadors or development workers to work within communities to disseminate the benefits of learning for older people.

- *Develop a set of pilot projects to test various approaches.*

  The pilots should serve as a guide to how governments could best practically implement a strategy for mainstreaming older people's learning.

Recommendations to older people

- *Start to believe in yourself, in your ability to learn and to teach others.*

- *Reject negative stereotypes of older people*; the greatest change in attitudes will come from older people themselves.

- *Be not afraid*: The last words, texted to his wife, by the late great poet, Seamus Heaney, were 'noli temere'; it is both an exhortation and a prayer. Older people have precious gifts to offer to us all.

- *Make the effort to find out about learning and education in your own area.*

  Most localities will offer some kinds of learning opportunities; make it your business to find out about them.

- *Team up with other older people to join programmes or start your own.*

  Older people working together are a powerful force and have the skills and experience to contribute to existing programmes or shape their own. Collaboration is surely the wise option.

- *Be good to yourselves, enhance your wellbeing and wisdom and enjoy yourselves.*

  Education might seem a bit daunting at first, but you will be surprised and delighted at how much you already know, your capacity for learning and how much fun learning can be.

- *Be good to society – share your learning, resilience and optimism with us.*

  You have so much to teach us all. Don't let the opportunity to make us wise slip away. Challenge the negative stereotypes and become active, insightful and 'cool' – a resource to us all.

Co-research as empowerment: our findings

As co-research was perhaps the most significant feature of this project from beginning to end, the last section of this book is focused on some of the important ideas which emerged, some of which were unexpected, but all of which were very welcome. There was no doubt that the process of co-research was empowering for everyone.

Motivation: why would older learners get involved in a co-research project?

Participants reported a range of motivating factors: some got involved because of a belief that the aims of the project were worthwhile; the co-researchers wanted to help other older learners and challenge negative stereotypes of older people. Allied to this was a desire to feel useful. For others, having the chance to voice their own views and hear those of others was considered important. The opportunity to exercise latent skills and knowledge, as well as gain new skills and knowledge, was welcomed. Again, this echoes the Madrid Plan (United Nations, 2002, unpaged), which recognises the contribution older people can play as mentors, mediators and advisers and the importance of utilising the social, cultural and educational knowledge potential of older learners.

Gains for older learners

The co-researchers reported a number of gains, including the satisfaction of seeing important research completed. Others gained satisfaction from using previous professional skills and acquiring new skills and knowledge, including learning and sharing ideas about 'old age' and 'retirement'. And for some, the opportunity to work with others was a benefit.

What older learners can give to a co-research project

Our team reflected that among the gifts they can bring to a research project are clear and enquiring minds and a task-focused or goal-centred approach. Some noted that they were able to bring ideas, personal stories and views based on experience, while others identified their contribution as time, energy, enthusiasm and skills. One student wildly understated the case when she conceded that older learners could bring 'a little wisdom'.

Time invested in co-research should be decided by the co-researchers

Participants recorded various amounts of time, from a few hours to 24 days or more. Since the project was deliberately set up to enable participants to engage in whatever way they wished, this was in turn reflected in the amount of time spent. It is to be noted that those who spent the most time seemed to gain the most from the project, so sustained involvement is likely to extend the degree of wellbeing and wisdom making. However, it must be acknowledged that not all learners can devote large amounts of time, or even wish to.

Training for and with co-researchers: how much training, what kinds of training?

Some participants did not believe that they needed training for their particular role in the project – for example, in setting up databases, organising interviewing schedules or creative documenting – as they already had these skills and volunteered to work on these aspects because they had those skills. Some participants who were interviewees may not have considered that they needed any training for this role. For those taking part as interviewers, data analysts and literature reviewers, training was viewed as important. Most who received training found it useful. Participants also appreciated the opportunity to be mentored in pilot interviews.

Co-research as a vehicle for drawing on and exercising existing skills and knowledge

Respondents overwhelmingly concluded that co-research did allow them to draw on existing skills – for example, interviewing or establishing rapport with other people. The co-researchers experienced the project as ratifying, as enabling them to re-use in a different context skills that they had thought now of no use to anybody.

Co-research as a vehicle for developing new skills and knowledge

The majority of respondents concluded that new skills were gained. New skills and knowledge identified included hearing different views in the learning process and learning that mature friends have so much to offer. One co-researcher testified that he had developed new skills in using modern computerised library databases as well as new knowledge about ageing from academic experts and cultural commentators.

Co-research can be a bit challenging

Some respondents concluded that there were some challenges, including dealing with different personalities, self-confidence at the start and the intellectual challenge of reading more and continuing to participate in courses. One of the creative documenters faced challenges in trying to photograph participants in confined and slightly artificial contexts. Others faced considerable challenges in having to learn about the huge amount literature relevant to the topic and how to express this in ways that had validity and meaning for a book.

Co-research is enjoyable

All respondents except one stated that there was no aspect of the process that they did not enjoy. Challenging it may have been, for some, but the challenge turned out to be a welcome exertion.

Co-research can sometimes, but not always, provide a means of developing networks

A majority of respondents concluded that networks were not developed, but some said that that they enjoyed being part of a team. In retrospect, I could have done more to foster networks, to create opportunities for the co-researchers to interact and reflect upon the process.

Co-research as a way of encouraging older learners to critically reflect on their learning programme

Our co-researchers concluded that participation in the co-research reiterated a positive approach to being involved in the programme, and confirmed their views about the advantages of being able to avail of the Open Learning Programme. Respondents appreciated the opportunity to articulate their views about their learning and to be empowered.

Co-research as a way of encouraging critical reflection on ageing and older people

Some responses noted that it was not just older people taking the courses, seeming, therefore, to question or even reject a focus on ageing. This reflects an ambivalence demonstrated in the findings and in the literature and may well be as a result of the negative impact of negative stereotypes upon older people themselves. Other respondents attested to how much more aware they became of aspects of ageing and older people, including: how varied older people are; how older people bring previous experience to bear; how old age is no joke; the continuing ability of older people to learn; the contribution older people can make to the 'mental capital' of the community; the benefits to wellbeing (emotional, mental and physical) from being involved in continuing education.

Participation in co-research can enhance wellbeing and wisdom

A majority of respondents believed that it can enhance wellbeing and wisdom. Benefits included: a sense of achievement; self-esteem and confidence; insight into different generations and a belief that participation in the research gave a great sense of contributing new insights to research into ageing and older people.

Being involved in co-research about older learners by older learners may contribute to challenging negative stereotypes

Respondents were divided on this, with about half saying that such research can challenge negative stereotypes. The somewhat doubtful sceptical response of some may go back to older people internalising negative stereotypes and an appreciation of the attitudinal mountain that has to be climbed.

Co-research projects with older people have the potential to help other older people

Almost all respondents believed that this was the case. Co-researchers said that the main benefits included adding to the knowledge base through discovering facts about ageing and learning, and becoming more aware of knowledge which can generate pride and positivity among older people. Others were of the view that such projects could encourage more people to get involved in learning and education and potentially influence policymakers and funders.

Once more into the breach? Engagement in one co-research project encourages older learners to do further projects

The co-researchers almost overwhelmingly agreed that this was the case. This is, indeed, encouraging and offers us all a challenge in terms of how we can further develop and enhance co-research projects with older learners.

Recommendations for co-research projects with older learners

These recommendations are for the most part addressed to policymakers, universities and other learning organisations, but they may also be of interest to older readers, who might be surprised to find that their contribution to research is a valuable commodity to society as a whole as well as being personally enhancing.

- *Ensure that the planned research has relevance and meaning for older students.*

  The rationale of the research needs to be grounded in what older students are actually interested in talking about and working on. This is not to say that older co-researchers could not be brought into a wide range of university research programmes. Indeed, thought needs to be given to how that might be achieved.

- *Ensure that the research has a purpose and a goal that is about benefiting society.*

  Older learners placed a high value on the ethos of the project; they were motivated to get involved because of an altruism which viewed participation as helping other older people and society more generally.

- *Respect and value the experience, knowledge and wisdom of the learners.*

  They are a vast, untapped resource. And older people are highly motivated to help, to be useful, to contribute.

- *Embed a co-research ethos at all levels of the research project – from steering group to interviewing, literature search and creative documentation.*

  This ensures a much fuller sense of empowerment for older researchers and also, crucially, enables them to enter the project on their own terms, choosing which role they wish to occupy, rather than being dragooned or stretched upon a Procrustean bed.

- *Deploy a range of research modes, including arts-based methods.*

  This will broaden the appeal of the project and enable project facilitators to draw on the range of skills and knowledge learners have.

- *Embed an ethos of trust, mutual respect, compassion and warmth.*

  Humanised and humanising research is far more likely to attract older people, who may well be intimidated initially by university research and perceptions that it is very abstract and way beyond them.

- *Provide training as appropriate, including training for interviewees.*

  This will vary according to the scale and complexity of the project, but opportunities for training definitely need to be available, to ensure that ethics standards are maintained but also to give older learners the new skills and confidence to embark on the research so that the research product is of high standard.

- *Offer expenses to participants.*

  Practice will vary from one organisation to another, and some universities and funders may well believe that older co-researchers should be paid at the 'market rate'. At the very least, participants should not be out of pocket and adequate expenses need to be offered.

- *Provide opportunities for participants to meet during and after the project.*

  In retrospect, while I did update participants by email, I believe that we should have offered more chances for the co-research team to meet, and for future projects I would advocate building in briefing seminars, perhaps with a cup of coffee. Not all participants may wish to attend or will have time, but the opportunity should be there.

- *Evaluate progress and embed flexibility to ensure that the project remains supple and responsive to co-researchers.*

  No project will ever go completely according to plan, and this needs to be urbanely accepted. Flexibility and adaptability are, therefore, crucial. Thus, for example, not all interviewers could attend the scheduled training session, so a further session was arranged. And, as it transpired, I needed more help with data analysis, literature review and editing than I had originally envisaged. But this was, it seems to me, something of a *felix culpa* or happy fault, since it paved the way for students to expand and extend their skills and to work as a small, very motivated team.

- *Disseminate research so that the profile and value of older people as researchers can be enhanced and negative stereotypes challenged.*

This book is a major way of doing just that. In the future, we plan to co-write articles and also, hopefully, to disseminate the research among older people's groups, policymakers and centres of ageing.

- *Try to ensure that the project is as enjoyable as possible.*

I can only hope that others engaging in co-research with older learners had as much fun as we had. While it is important to maintain a serious-ness of purpose, it is preferable not to become too solemn, to keep per-spective and to have an odd good laugh at ourselves; that is the ultimate wisdom of the elders.

A final word

From the data gathered in this small co-research project on the Open Learn-ing Programme at Queen's University Belfast, I would conclude that our older learners are distinguished; they bother to read books or learn deeply about the practical skills involved in guitar playing or figuring out a train timetable in German. To put this another way, they bring to whatever subject they choose to study a seriousness of purpose, a curiosity, an intensity and a will-ingness to become sagacious. Our older learners were once young too and subject to the pressures of the career-filled world. But what they can teach us – these distinguished learners – is quite simply the benefits of a love of learn-ing in itself. This pursuit of learning is there when you are in pain or at a loss, when nothing else is there, whether you are young or old; it is a mark of your resilience, your refusal to be 'done in' by the slings and arrows of outrageous fortune – a consolation, a joy. Is that not something worth teaching? Have not older learners a message for the younger generation? Might it be that older people can offer to the young a way out of their sense of helplessness and meaninglessness, their sense of being powerless victims or automatons caught in the machine of relentless corporatised 'performance' – a bracing, humorous, challenging, questing spirit? For older people have, indeed, seen, if not it all, then something not dissimilar and know that the only way out of loss is what they have finally managed to do – learn for dear life. Might our older learners not sagaciate us all with their creativity, as seen in student Charles Brannigan's drawings, Figures 6.1 and 6.2, and through their grit, registering the past and looking forward to tomorrow, as seen in Figure 6.3.

Figure 6.1 Near the home of the Blackbird Bookclub, one of the Open Learning courses.

Figure 6.2 Door into the light.

Figure 6.3 Figuring the past and the future; laughing it all away.

References

Aldridge, F. and Hughes, D. (2012) *Adult participation in learning survey*, Leicester: NIACE.

BeLL Project. (2014) 'About the project' [online]. Available at http://www.bell-project. eu/cms/ (Accessed: 3 July 2015).

Benyson, J., Börger, A., Briguglio, G., Cicollela, F., Cosgrove, A., D'Angelo, M., Danihelkova, H., Devine, S., Drobna, D., Galisova, L., Grabowska, A., Hale, C., Hanelova, K., Hinterberger, M., Kurz, R., Mastroeni, C., Rose, G. and Soulsby, J. (2010) *Getting older people involved in learning: The EuBIA guide*, Graz, Austria: EuBIA [online]. Available at https://www2.le.ac.uk/departments/lifelong-learning/ research/LLAG/research/images/eubia-guide-en.pdf (Accessed: 2 July 2015).

Boulton-Lewis, G. (2012) 'Issues in learning and education for the ageing', in Boulton-Lewis, G. and Tam, M. (eds.) *Active ageing, active learning: Issues and challenges* (Education in the Asia-Pacific Region: Issues, Concerns and Prospects), New York: Springer, pp. 21–34.

Brady, E.M., Cardale, A. and Neidy, J.C. (2013) 'The quest for community in Osher lifelong learning institutes', *Educational, Gerontology*, 39 (9), pp. 627–639.

Davies, R. (2014) 'Older people in Europe: EU policies and programmes', *European Parliamentary Research Service Briefing*, 6 May, 2014, pp. 1–8. Available at http://www.europarl.europa.eu/RegData/bibliotheque/briefing/2014/140811/ LDM_BRI(2014)140811_REV1_EN.pdf (Accessed: 27 December 2015).

European Commission. (undated) 'Education and training: Supporting education and training in Europe and beyond', Brussels: European Commission. Available at http://ec.europa.eu/education/ (Accessed: 27 December 2015).

Field, J. (2009) *Well-being and happiness – inquiry into the future for lifelong learning, IFLL Thematic Paper 4*, Leicester: NIACE.

Field, J. (2012) 'Lifelong learning, welfare and mental well-being into older age: Trends and policies in Europe', in Boulton-Lewis, G. and Tam, M. (eds.) *Active ageing, active learning: Issues and challenges* (Education in the Asia-Pacific Region: Issues, Concerns and Prospects), New York: Springer, pp. 11–19.

Findsen, B. (2005) *Learning later*, Malabar, FL: Kreiger Publishing Company.

Findsen, B. (2014) 'Older adult education in a New Zealand university: Developments and issues', *International Journal of Education and Ageing*, 3 (3), 211–224.

Findsen, B., McCullough, S. and McEwan, B. (2011) 'Later life learning for adults in Scotland: Tracking the engagement with and impact of learning for working-class men and women', *International Journal of Lifelong Education*, 30 (4), pp. 527–547.

Future Foundation. (2014) *The Future of loneliness: Facing the challenge of loneliness for older people in the UK, 2014–2030*, London: Future Foundation/Friends of the Elderly.

Hyde, M. and Phillipson, C. (2014) *How can lifelong learning, including continuous training within the labour market, be enabled and who will pay for this? Looking forward to 2025 and 2040 and how this might evolve?*, London: Government Office for Science and Foresight. Available at https://www.gov.uk/government/ uploads/system/uploads/attachment_data/file/463059/gs-15–9-future-ageing-lifelong-learning-er02.pdf (Accessed: 27 December 2015).

Leamy, M. and Clough, R. (2006) *How older people became researchers: Training, guidance and practice in action*, York: Joseph Rowntree Foundation.

Lee, Y., Wei, H. and Hu, M. (2014) 'An exploration in the learning processes of retirees in Singapore', *Contemporary Educational Research Quarterly*, 22 (3), pp. 91–30.

Nash, I. (2015) 'Politicians must start seeing lifelong learning as an investment – not a cost', *The Guardian*, 9 March, unpaged. Available at http://www.theguardian.com/education/2015/mar/09/adult-education-funding-cuts-lifelong-learning-investment (Accessed: 22 December 2015).

Nolan, P. (2007) *Adult learning in Northern Ireland: An overview of current policies and practice. A briefing paper for NIACE*, Leicester: NIACE.

Northern Ireland Council for Voluntary Action. (2015) *The fiscal implications of an older population in Northern Ireland*, Belfast: NICVA, The Centre for Economic Empowerment and the New policy Institute. Available at http://www.nicva.org/sites/default/files/d7content/attachments-resources/cee_report_12_the_fiscal_implications_of_an_older_population_in_northern_ireland.pdf (Accessed: 27 December 2015).

Office of the First Minister and Deputy First Minister [Northern Ireland Assembly]. (2014) *Active ageing strategy, 2014–2020: Consultation document*, Belfast: Office of the First Minister and Deputy First Minister [Northern Ireland Assembly]. Available at https://www.ofmdfmni.gov.uk/sites/default/files/consultations/ofmdfm_dev/active-ageing-strategy-2014-2020-consultation.pdf (Accessed: 26 December 2015).

Schuller, T. and Watson, D. (2009) *Learning through life: Inquiry into the future for lifelong learning*, Leicester: NIACE.

Segal, L. (2013) *The pleasures and the perils of ageing: Out of time*, London, NY: Verso.

Staehelin, H.B. (2005) 'Promoting health and wellbeing in later life', in Johnson, M.L. (ed.) *The Cambridge handbook on age and ageing*, Cambridge: Cambridge University Press, pp. 165–180.

Steptoe, A., Deaton, A. and Stone, A. (2015) 'Subjective wellbeing, health, and ageing', *The Lancet*, 385 (9968), pp. 640–648.

Trowler, P. and Trowler, V. (2010) *Student engagement evidence summary*, York: Higher Education Academy.

Tuckett, A. (2014) *Seriously useless learning: The collected TES writings of Alan Tuckett*, Nash, I. (ed.), Leicester: NIACE.

UK Department of Health. (2013) *Government response to the house of lords select committee on public service and demographic change report of session 2012–13: 'Ready for ageing?'*, London: Department of Health.

United Nations. (2002) *Political declaration and Madrid international plan of action on ageing*, Madrid: Second World Assembly on Ageing, Madrid, Spain, 8–12 April, New York: United Nations. Available at http://www.un.org/en/events/pastevents/pdfs/Madrid_plan.pdf (Accessed: 27 December 2015).

Von Radowitz, J. (2014) 'Pensioners with purpose live longer', *I Newspaper*, 6th November, p. 19.

Withnal, A. (2004) 'Older learners: Challenging the myths', in Withnal, A., McGivney, V. and Soulsby, J. (eds.) *Older people learning – myths and realities*, Leicester: NIACE, pp. 85–100.

Withnal, A. and Percy, K. (1994) *Good practice in the education and training of older adults*, Aldershot, Hants.: Ashgate Publishing Ltd. Available at http://www.uni-ulm.de/LiLL/5.0/E/5.3/practice.html (Accessed: 13 August 2015).

Appendix I

Course evaluation form

QUEEN'S UNIVERSITY BELFAST

SCHOOL OF EDUCATION (OPEN LEARNING) – SPRING 2014

COURSE EVALUATION FORM

We are keen to know your opinion of the course you have taken. Your answers will help improve the quality of the learning experience for future students. Please complete this course evaluation form and return it to the Tutor before leaving the final session. Please **do not** reveal your identity on the form.

Course Code: OLE1772 **Course Name:** The Blackbird Book

Course Tutor: Tess Maginess

Where did you find out about course: Mailing List/Friend/Newspaper/Library/Web/Other.....................
(Please circle as appropriate)

	Agree Strongly	Agree	Not Sure	Disagree	Disagree Strongly
1. I enjoyed the course					
2. The course was well organised					
3. The amount and level of difficulty of material covered in the course was about right					
4. The tutor was approachable for help					
5. I would recommend this course to a friend					
6. I think the course was good value for money					
FOR THOSE COMPLETING CREDIT BEARING ASSESSMENT WORK					
7. I found the assessment useful					
8. Details of the assessment were adequately explained					
9. Feedback from tutors on assessment work was good					

Any general comments you would like to add (for example what you have enjoyed, something to be altered, what you would like to do next)

THANK YOU FOR COMPLETING THIS QUESTIONNAIRE. PLEASE RETURN TO COURSE TUTOR.

Figure A.1 Course evaluation form: Queen's University Belfast, School of Education (Open Learning) – spring 2014.

Appendix 2

Special courses on ageing

Tutor evaluation form (questions to be asked in filmed interview)

1 What was your initial response to being involved in one of the special courses on ageing?
2 What kind of response did you get from the students to the topic of old age?
3 What kind of response did you get about the material you presented?
4 Are you learning anything from the students about older people?
5 Do you think that facilitating this course will deepen your understanding of older people?
6 Do you think this project will enhance the wellbeing of the learners?

Appendix 3

Interview questions

1 What is it about the Open Learning Programme that you like best?
2 Why did you enrol on Open Learning? What course (s) did you enrol on? Why did you choose this/these particular course (s)?

   a Did you enrol on one of the 'special' courses to do with ageing? If not, can you tell us why? If you did enrol, can you tell us why?
   b Did the special course meet your expectations? What did you take away from it?

3 Have you made many friends through Open Learning? If so, can you tell me about that?
4 What have you learned through the Open Learning Programme – any new skills or knowledge? Do you find these useful?
5 What do you think of the way you are taught, the learning and teaching styles?
6 Do you talk to your family or friends about the course? Do you recommend any family or friends to enrol? If so why?
7 What do you think of the support staff and services (e.g. for disabled people)?
8 Are there any barriers or reasons that stand in the way of enrolling or attending the course?
9 Is there anything that you would like to change about the programme you enrolled in?
10 Are there courses that you would like to see in the programme? Do you think there should be special courses about ageing each year?
11 Do you think the courses are good value for money? Could you elaborate on that?
12 What do you think are the main advantages for older people engaging in lifelong learning?
13 (a) How did you enrol on the Open Learning Programme (Online, postal, telephone, in person)? (b) How did you find out about the programme?

Additional comments

Please add any additional comments here:

Appendix 4

Questionnaire to volunteer participants

Dear participants,

Firstly, let me thank you all most sincerely for getting involved in the project about older learners. Could I impose a little further on your good nature by asking you to complete this questionnaire? The results (anonymous, unless you indicate that you would like to be named) will be used in the book about the project, which is being published by Routledge and which I am currently writing. Filling out the questionnaire would be a great help as you may be able to point the way forward for other older learners. Thank you very much.

Tess

1 Why did you agree to be involved?
2 In what capacity were you involved? Circle as appropriate (you can circle more than one):

> *Member of the steering group*
> *Organiser – e.g. compiling a database for the project, creating models for interview scheduling*
> *Participant in one of the special courses on ageing*
> *Peer tutor in one of the special courses on ageing*
> *Interviewee*
> *Interviewer*
> *Data analyst*
> *Helping with the literature review*
> *As a creative documenter – e.g. photography or illustration*

3 What did you think at the beginning that you would get out of being involved in the project?
4 What did you think you would be able to give to it when you began?
5 How much time did you spend on the project?
6 Were you offered expenses?
7 If you received training, how useful was it? How could it have been improved?

8 Was your involvement in the project what you expected? If not, how did it differ?

9 What did you learn from being involved – about yourself, about what you now think about older learners, older people?

10 Were you able to draw on skills/knowledge you had developed in an earlier part of your life?

11 Did you learn new skills/knowledge?

12 Did your involvement in the project challenge you? If so, how?

13 Was there any aspect of your involvement that you did not like?

14 Did you develop any social networks/friendships through being involved?

15 Do you think your involvement contributed to or enhanced your wellbeing and wisdom? If so, how?

16 Do you think, by being involved, you have contributed to challenging negative stereotypes of older people?

17 Do you think this project could help other older people? If so, how?

18 Would you like to do more projects like this? If so, how would you like to be involved?

19 Additional comments: please free to elaborate on any of your answers above or add further comments.

Index

Page numbers for figures are in italics.